My Boyfriend is a Twat

My Boyfriend
is a Twat

A guide to recognising, dealing
and living with an utter Twat

Zoe McCarthy

FRIDAY
BOOKS

First published in Great Britain in 2007 by Friday Books
An imprint of The Friday Project Limited
83 Victoria Street, London SW1H 0HW

www.thefridayproject.co.uk
www.fridaybooks.co.uk

Text © 2007 Zoe McCarthy
www.myboyfriendisatwat.com

Line Illustrations © 2007 Lucy Pepper
www.lucypepper.com/blogzira

ISBN – 13   978-1-905548-58-3

British Library Cataloguing in Publication Data

A catalogue record for this book is available from the
British Library

Cover design by Snowbooks Design
Internal design, additional illustrations and typesetting by e-Digital Design
Printed by MPG Books Ltd

The Publisher's policy is to use paper manufactured from
sustainable sources

For Andy

With thanks to...

Andy Hopkins and Joanna M., my 'little helpers',
to all my friends for their support and encouragement,
The Friday Project, Lorna Read and most of all,
my boyfriend, the twat in my life.

Contents

As I lit my Amnesty International candle on AI Day
at work, the Intern asked me what it was for.

"It's a candle in remembrance of all those people suffering
and being tortured all around the world," I replied.

"Yes," added the Twat, "and I think of myself every day."

Introduction

Living with the opposite species is hard enough as it is, but when your Significant Other just happens to be a complete and utter twat as well, it really makes the going get tough. I have coupled up with quite a few planks in my time, not out of choice, mind, but out of sheer bad character judgment, so you may as well say that it is entirely my fault. So, when asked if I would compile a manual about recognising, dealing and coping with a complete and utter twat, I wondered if this was to add insult to injury as to my choice in men, or a desperate call for help. I mulled it over and finally agreed, thinking that it would be an easy task to take on. Wrong. This has to be the most difficult thing anyone has ever asked me to do, especially as living with a twat makes life all the more difficult. Indeed, so far the only help he has given me is advice on how I *should* have written this book and several cups of coffee.

Don't get me wrong. I love my boyfriend incredibly, which confuses him no end, but hey, he's just a simple lad and he is trying. Oh yes, he's very trying indeed. I gave up expressing my feelings to my boyfriend a long time ago as every time I said, "I love you," he would always reply with "Who's this Hugh chap?" So, if you think that I am being in any way harsh by categorising him as a twat, then you really don't know the man.

If nothing else, this book is intended as a guide to help all of you out there who are about to throw yourselves into a relationship to stop, consider and take a good look at the person with whom you so badly want to share your life, as you could be about to make the Biggest Mistake Ever. I don't regret my decision to take a twat under my roof; in fact, he has made a rather interesting contribution to my household and for that I thank him. It's the rest of the things that he does that I don't thank him for, such as breathing. And farting. Especially the farting. What can you do when you live with a man whose idea of cultural sensitivity is being able to fart along to the Belgian National Anthem? Or who thinks of me as someone who: every 28 days has her period, every 21 days renews *A Suitable Boy* at the library and every 1,825 days gets her coil replaced?

Recognising a twat can be fairly simple, but dealing and coping with one has made me, on more than one occasion, want to opt for childbirth again, were the option to arise.

A twat is not necessarily a bad thing to be. Some people just can't help themselves. But it can be very painful for all those who have to put up with a twat. They are often warm and loving people who just happen to have twattish tendencies that make you turn around and say, "You *TWAT!*" at the top of your voice. Many of the twats I know are also extremely well-travelled, well-read and incredibly intelligent, but none of those qualities alienate a twat from doing the most stupid to the most absurd actions.

By now, you may well be asking yourself, "What is a stupid or an absurd action?" That is the exact reason why you are reading this book, as it is filled with shining examples of just why My Boyfriend is a Twat.

The Twat

INTRODUCING THE TWAT

Before going any further with this book, it is only fair that I should introduce you to the Twat and perhaps give you a few home truths about who he is. Not that this in any way means that the rest of the book is fictitious as, sadly enough, it is entirely based on fact.

Place of Birth: it was clearly in a barn as no hospital would take him after the psychics warned the midwife of his future stays in hospitals dotted around the world, for all sorts of reasons. He claims that he was found on a fell in Cumbria under a pile of sheep dung, left on top of him by a passing sheep to keep the warmth in. He must have been found by fell-walkers who couldn't stand the screeching sound of a baby as they settled down to eat their bacon butties after a strenuous walk up the fell.

Having said that, I don't think it is necessarily true, but the Twat's sticking to it.

Education: this is a grey area as the Twat couldn't even find his way out of the house, let alone the bus route to school. On a bad day, he made it to school and caused havoc. On a good day, he played truant, leaving school with few qualifications – although credit is due to him in that he followed up on IT studies and, ever since, has hated Bill Gates with a passionate loathing only matched by that of Lady Diana for Camilla Parker-Bowles.

Vital Statistics (these days): rather large, even larger, unevenly smaller.

Height: he says 5'10". I say 5'5".

Weight: 85 kilos, depending on the day.

Eyes: two, blue.

Hair colour: mousy brown and the odd grey hair.

Birthday: October 17.

Born: eight months before me.

Starsign: the dreaded Libra.

Occupation: part-time IT manager and web-designer when thrown at him. His real passion is in conservation, building dry stone walls and footpaths in the fells in Cumbria, Shropshire and Tanzania, which is where he was named 'Quarsan' by the Iraqw tribe. There are three reasons for this name. Number one: Quarsan means 'a man who can do many things', although I think that the Iraqw tribe really got that one wrong. Secondly, he was so-called after a tribal leader who led the Iraqw tribe to where they are based now. The tribal leader lived on the escarpment where Quarsan was working, and, like the Twat, the leader loved mountains. Thirdly, there was a man in the neighbouring village who was also called Quarsan and they looked very much alike. According to the Twat, it was all down to bone stucture and, when tanned, he doesn't look that different from a pale African. Seeing as the Iraqw tribe originated from Mesopotamia, Iraq, they were considered 'white Africans'. Personally, I'm beginning to wonder if the Twat hasn't done a 'Michael Jackson' and is trying very hard to explain the different shades of brown that exist. He's a bloke. Brown is brown or, to be politically correct, black is black.

Interests: reading, staying immobile for as long as possible, eating, politics, computers, photography and taking the piss out of me.

EARLY DAYS OF TWATDOM

WHERE WAS I?

I had moved over to Belgium by mistake. Oh yes, there is more than one idiot in this household and I am not talking about my son. Under some unfortunate circumstances that most twenty-year-olds go through, my father was not very pleased with my choice of boyfriend. And so he sent me back to England from his then posting abroad, with instructions not to contact my brothers or any other relatives that I may have known of.

England is a country that I don't know particularly well. I spent a great deal of time in boarding school (okay, only nine years, but that was enough) and I never learnt much about the town that I was in as we were only let out once every term, for just one hour. Yes, that's how I got to know England. When I finally left school, I attended an awful crash-course in Secretarial Studies somewhere in Oxford. I managed to achieve the lightning speed of 50 words per minute in shorthand, even though I could never read my notes afterwards.

So I left. For Belgium – it's small, my parents had already been posted here and so I knew it all. Well, I thought I did. In fact,

I am only just discovering Belgium now, after about 22 years in this country. I love the quirkiness of this small country which has been invaded by just about every other nation, sometimes by more than one at the same time. Despite Belgium's size it has still managed to provoke a lot of hatred, especially between the Dutch-speaking Flemings and the French-speaking Walloons. Elections here are rather confusing because if you live in Flanders, the Dutch-speaking area of Belgium, you find yourself voting for Flemish MPs only, and presumably the same applies in Wallonia where you can only vote for French-speaking MPs. And that's just a taste of this country. It appeals to me because it makes me laugh, and I get very annoyed with people who slag this country off or say things like, "I bet you can't name ten famous Belgians... " Because I can. So there.

I married a Belgian, then divorced him, then married another, then divorced him, had a couple of flings and then...

HOW?
I met Quarsan over the internet, via a Bulletin Board that I originally used to look up some information about Phuket as I was about to spend ten short days there. He was witty, daft

and his chat-up line was, "Would you like a cream bun?" The man obviously had a long way to go, and the further, the better. So he went to Tanzania for a few years to do some more footpath restoration.

During his time in Tanzania, we carried on corresponding via email and online chatting, thanks to the power of the internet, whenever he escaped out of the little village where he lived in search of a hot curry in Arusha, or perhaps a Chinese meal – just anything but the usual boring beans and rice. The other plus side was that there was electricity on a steady basis in Arusha.

I enjoyed having a pen-pal and his stories from the Bush were always a treat. He would often send me pictures of where he lived and the work that he was doing, as well as his friends, his house-girl and her baby, opening up a completely new window in my tiny world. He finally returned to England when he learnt of his father's death about a week late, but then news doesn't travel fast in Africa. When things had settled down again, he was back on the Bulletin Board keeping everybody updated with what was going on in the TV series, *Big Brother*.

That year, a bunch of friends of mine invited me over to London for a party and seeing as I had the spare cash, for once, I decided to take up their invitation. Quarsan caught wind of the fact that I was visiting London – I probably told him, to be honest – and decided that he wanted to meet me. The only problem there was the fact that I didn't want to meet him. He was my pen-pal, not somebody who I actually wanted to get to know in person, and besides, he spent half his time in the Lake District and the other half in Africa. And what if he was an axe-wielding murderer? It was bad enough that he was, and still is, a Northerner. I was taking a huge risk.

WHERE?

It only took the man two weeks to persuade me to meet up with him. We decided to get together on the Saturday, after which I'd join my friends. I agreed to meet him at Euston Station where we recognised each other straight away and said 'wow' a lot. We drank lots of coffee and then spent a couple of hours in a pub, where Quarsan gave me a book about the Lake District and a kilo of Cumberland sausages. I should have guessed from the sausages as to what sort of a man he was, but it was too late. We'd fallen for each other.

AND THEN?

When the time came, we went our separate ways, although it has to be said that Quarsan was so smitten by my beautiful self that he jumped into the taxi and asked for King's Cross station, rather than back to Euston. I have this effect on people sometimes. I went on to the party clutching a book and that kilo of Cumberland sausages, which drew quite a bit of attention. After I returned home, the Twat visited on a couple of occasions, decided that he liked Belgium and moved in.

Naturally, I asked my children if he could live with us and we came to a decision that if ever any one of us was unhappy with Quarsan's presence then they should say so. As it happened, the kids took to him like bees to a honey pot, and although the Twat has never fathered a child to his knowledge, he befriended the children straight away. Several years later and he still hasn't asked if he can stay, as he is still thinking about it.

THE WEBLOG?

I noticed that the Twat used to spend an awful lot of time on his laptop until one day the screen went black for good. After that, he used my computer rather a lot and I noticed that he had something called a 'weblog' that was incredibly boring as it was mainly about politics. Nevertheless, he used to link to other people's weblogs, as this was obviously a very fashionable thing to do. There were a couple that the Twat linked to that I very much liked and would visit myself on a daily basis. They were fun, amusing, well-written – and still are.

One day, as we came out of the supermarket and I yet again told him that he was 'a twat!' for having gone there without the shopping list that had been so carefully put together by yours-truly, he replied, ever so simply, and perhaps in jest – but I highly doubt that – that I should set up a weblog called *My Boyfriend is a Twat*. Stupid move.

"OK, I will. I don't understand a thing so you set it up for me," I said.

"Awright, hun," he agreed, and even bought me my own domain name for Valentine's Day the following year.

And hence the birth of the Twat.

And that is exactly where the beginning of this book lies. The weblog is mainly rants about my household, which has been described by a friend as a mixture of *The Osbournes*, *Absolutely Fabulous* and *My Family*. When my friend said this, he meant it in all seriousness, and let's face it, it's bleeding obvious.

The household is made up of five people. There's myself, Zoe, an oasis of calm and my boyfriend, Quarsan, aka the Twat. (Let's face it, girls, all men are twats, but Quarsan takes the biscuit and here's his reward!).

Then there is Amber, an 18-year-old stroppy little cow, her twin sister, Hazel, who bosses the Twat and me around and winds up their brother Jake, a 14-year-old with the attention span of a gnat, plus, of course, the occasional pets which have, over the years, included one cat (dead), two rabbits (both dead), a hamster (dead) and three goldfish, of which two are officially dead and one still survives.(Actually, all three of the originals are dead. I was goldfish-sitting while the girls were away and Hazel's fish died so I replaced it. She still doesn't know.)

KNOWING ME, KNOWING THE TWAT

Since I started my website in 2003, several people who leave comments appear to have actually met Quarsan, not to mention the fact that he once lived opposite another blogger's local pub. One of the people who knew him when they both lived in Edinburgh, now lives in Australia, but via the strange and wonderful powers of the internet they met up again via my site. Somebody else who now lives in Nigeria used to pilot the RAF helicopter that the Twat flew on when he was doing Mountain Rescue, and yet another person once emailed me asking whether or not my boyfriend knew a certain man called Simon and it turned out that Simon was a mutual friend of theirs. Pure coincidence? Or a case of the Twat leaving an indelible impression everywhere he goes?

During his first ever visit to Morocco, a string of events has led me to wonder if the Twat isn't jinxed in some way...

The Twat and his best mate, Dan, were in Tafroute, Morocco, a small village in the Anti Atlas mountains. It has a steady tourist trade, but it's very low key and often there are no more than half a dozen travellers in the town.

The first encounter with the Twat's past was when he and Dan met a young Scottish woman called Sue who was staying in the same hotel. They got chatting and the three of them decided to spend the following day out together, walking to the boulders just outside town. They thought it would be fun to camp overnight there as many of the large boulders had been painted by some Belgian artist, which made the visit all the more interesting. They each packed sleeping bags, a camping stove, water and food and it wasn't till they sat down for a bit of lunch that Sue and the Twat realised they had history in common. Sue lived in Edinburgh, as did the Twat in the '80s. Not much of a real coincidence there, until they discovered that Sue's boyfriend was the Twat's old flatmate, when he lived in Leith.

As they mused over the strange piece of synchronicity, eating fresh bread and 'laughing cow cheese', a cheery voice shouted out, "Hello there".

A middle-aged bloke wearing a huge floppy hat wandered over and introduced himself as Bob who lived in Keswick, about 15 minutes' drive away from where Quarsan and Dan lived in Ambleside. It wasn't long before it was established that the Twat had met Bob before, and they had a lot of mutual acquaintances through none other than the Mountain Rescue Team…

Rather goosed from these strange coincidences in such an out of the way place, they decided that heading back to town to drink coffee was the best way of recovering.

Once they got back to the Hotel Tangier, they found an Irish guy sitting outside having a brew. They started chatting, as you do, and, well, the Twat didn't know this guy personally, but he had just had a house-guest for the week prior to the holiday. The Twat's house-guest was from Wicklow, as was the guy in the café.

"I've just got to ask…" began the Twat.

Would you believe, not only did the Irishman know Quarsan's house-guest, he grew up in the house next door to him, and had a photo of said house-guest and their mutual mates in his wallet. Beware, travel with the Twat and his past will catch up with you…

Another story from the Twat's past doesn't involve him directly, but does show how horribly small this world is. During his first stay in the hospital in the Bush in Tanzania (see the section on Twat Health for the gory details), there happened to be an American-Greek girl working there as a volunteer, basically to get away from her tight-knit family back in America. It was her first time abroad and she was desperate to stay away from home for as long as possible.

So desperate was she not to go home that whenever she did something wrong, she'd burst into tears and beg not to be sent back to her family as they would only marry her off to a shepherd. Feeling sorry for her, the Twat tried talking to her while she was changing the bandage on his foot. He started off by asking where she came from.

"Oh, please don't ask me that," was the reply. "Everybody does. I come from a small Greek island."

"Oh? Which one?"

"Really, you wouldn't know it. Nobody does and nobody has ever heard of it."

"Go on," urged the Twat, not renowned for knowing when to stop.

"No, no – it's just one of the small ones. Really, you would never have heard of it."

"Please, why don't you just tell me where you are from?" insisted the Twat.

The volunteer nurse sighed. "Alright, but you won't have heard of it. I come from Evvia."

"Really?" asked the Twat. "Are you from Pefki or Khalkis?"

"Khalkis, but how on earth do you know the place?" replied the startled girl. "You are the first person outside of Greece who has heard of my island."

"My sister is married to a Greek and they happen to live in Pefki..."

Knowing Quarsan is like playing *Six Degrees of Kevin Bacon* which, according to Wikipedia, 'was invented in 1994 as a play on the concept: the goal is to link any actor to Kevin Bacon through no more than six connections, where two

actors are connected if they have appeared in a movie together.'
Or even, *Six Degrees of Separation* which, says Wikipedia
again, 'refers to the idea that if you are one "step" away from
each person you know, then you are two "steps" away from
each person who is known by one of the people you know,
and you are no more than six "steps" away from each person
on earth.'

Via knowing my partner, I have found that I am two steps away
from Kylie Minogue and although I have great admiration for the
popstar, those are two steps too close as far as I am concerned,
due to his obsession with her.

Having a boyfriend who appears to be known by
everybody on earth can actually be off-putting and
make you feel rather inferior. Well, it used to make me
feel that way. Unless your partner is a famous
celebrity, then there is no reason to feel inferior at
all. Just tell people that "he gets around a bit"
and you'll see that your partner will soon
start paying more attention to you
than to those ghosts from his past.

ADJUSTING TO BELGIUM

CULTURE SHOCK

You can take a man out of Cumbria but there is no way in hell that you can take Cumbria out of a man.

The Twat is a well-travelled person, having visited quite a bit of the Middle East and Africa in particular. Each visit abroad has always been an experience, many of which are medical, bumping into old friends, getting Africans drunk, or simply doing his thing. Nothing, I think, quite prepared him for his decision to move to Belgium though and, in hindsight, I reckon it must have been a decision made on the spur of the moment. It certainly came as a surprise to me when he mentioned it.

The first obvious problem was a linguistic one: the Twat neither speaks French nor Flemish/Dutch, and some could say that his English isn't that great, either. Both French and Flemish/Dutch are spoken in Belgium and the Twat has managed to come this far mainly by gesticulating. When he's in the company of French-speakers, my boyfriend's French will deteriorate badly if I am there as he relies on me to translate – and the French speakers rely on me, too, as making head or tail of what on earth the man is trying to say can be difficult, if not impossible. He did try learning French for a short while, but the most he ever did was sit at the back of the class making friends with Iranian diplomats – and talking about Iran. And before you ask, yes, he has been there.

The second obvious problem was the culture. The Twat has never had any trouble living abroad, but he has only experienced living in Tanzania, Gambia and England and knows very little about Europeans. Not being able to have a debit card to withdraw money until he had a place of residence and an identity card, caused the Twat to ruffle up his feathers on countless occasions. Although strangely enough, for an Englishman, he didn't complain too much about having to obtain an ID card, especially the simple one delivered to him that has to be renewed on a regular basis. His only objection, in fact, was that it doesn't fit into his wallet and, naturally, the card had only been in his possession for just over a year before he lost it.

As my boyfriend hardly knows Europe, he was far from ready to find himself living in a country where the shops are shut on Sundays and the offices are very fond of their bank holidays. During the Twat's first year here, he found himself getting very frustrated due to the lackadaisical lifestyle that the Belgians appear to have adopted. I very clearly remember the Twat getting into the car one Saturday announcing that he was just popping round to see his doctor for a prescription renewal as he had run out of Ventolin. I replied by saying that you have to make an appointment first, and besides, it being a Saturday, the doctor wouldn't be at the clinic. Not only that but, unless he could find a pharmacy 'on call', or was prepared to venture into the centre of town, he'd be out of luck as most pharmacies are shut over the weekends.

Furious, the Twat got out of the car and decided to take out his anger by kicking it. Several hours later, he took up my suggestion of going to ER to get his prescription, came back and promptly forgot all about it till Monday. Some things are better left unsaid.

Should your partner be moving from another country to live with you, it is always wise to prepare him as much as possible for any inevitable shocks. Such as shops being shut on Sundays, doctors who don't make home-calls and even a different language. If there is an

English language magazine in the country that is specifically aimed at ex-pats, then that is what you need to get him. Whether he reads it or not isn't your problem as you will have done your bit. You can only help a man so much and if he doesn't follow your advice, it will be his loss entirely and then it is up to you to make him know that by refusing to have sex with him for about a year.

Mistranslate for him, send him to the wrong places and he'll soon learn.

Trust me.

FOREIGN PHONES

Having spent many previous years on top of a mountain throwing rocks around in Cumbria, Quarsan had led a pretty simple life. He had shared a house with several other people, knew the entire village, went climbing and drank coffee. Never in his 38 years had he had the need for a mobile phone, nor had he ever ventured inside the world that is called IKEA.

Things were about to change drastically. As I tried to prepare a welcome for my partner, I thought it would be a good idea to set him up with a mobile phone as well. I may just as well have given a chimpanzee a hard disk to play around with. The Twat was baffled by this small piece of technology, which he soon came to nick-name 'Zoe's boyfriend-tracker', and it has become about as mobile as a 10-ton stone. It's only on rare occasions that he has his phone with him, although he does use it a lot to send text messages to his mate in the UK, especially when in a restaurant.

If you are about to invite somebody into your life who has spent a large part of his life living in a small village where electricity is a luxury and running water has yet to be heard of, then be ready to transform yourself into your future partner's mother. It won't last long, as normally he will be absolutely fascinated by these luxuries, although give him time to work out how to use the phone. And call him regularly so as to get him used to it. It isn't a bad idea to buy your future partner a toy phone to help him get used to the concept first.

DRIVING ABROAD

Driving was another small hurdle, but the Twat soon got used to driving on the right-hand side of the road, despite the fact that the first time we used the car to go to the local supermarket, some idiot backed into us. At the time, the car was not yet ours, we were just borrowing it. Needless to say, it was a bit of an embarrassment telling the owner that we had just been rear-ended. When stuck in a traffic jam, or behind some lousy driver, the Twat's language would suddenly become extremely aggressive and there have been times when I have almost got out of the car in the middle of nowhere to escape the tension.

The Twat can get extremely frustrated when driving, especially when lost. I have told him on numerous occasions to pull over at the next garage and ask for directions, but it's obviously a bloke-thing; asking for directions shows failure in getting from A to B, and besides, it's always my fault for not having read the map properly.

If you can drive, then do all the driving as it's far more therapeutic for you to be able to swear and blame your

partner in the event of getting lost. On the other hand, many men tend to take the piss out of female drivers and if you end up with a gobshite of a partner who moans about your driving, parking skills and anything else that goes on behind the wheel, then there is only one solution: stop the car and force him to get out. Then speed off before he can so much as turn around and give you the royal finger.

DISCOVERING BELGIUM

However much the Twat may grumble about this country, about the flatness of it and how boring the countryside is, the things he finds to amuse himself with never fail to amaze me. When our car was still running, the Twat found it incredible that he could, if he fancied, visit five different countries in one day without either having a passport or having to change currency. In fact, you can visit three of those five countries and speak French in all three of them, although it is one of the Twat's major achievements that he manages to get by with speaking English in any European country, including France. He simply plays the village idiot again, which is neither a hard task for him nor is it far from the truth. To be fair, I would liken the Twat to the common court jester, but he does admit to playing the village idiot himself, so I'll let that one be.

As Belgium is not renowned for its mountains, Quarsan had to hang up his rope and crampons in the garage and basically say farewell to his climbing days, even though there are some bits of rock in the Ardennes that people climb. However, those are made of limestone and the man doesn't like climbing limestone, claiming that it reminds him of Yorkshire. Instead, the Twat took to discovering Brussels and taking photos of 'strange' buildings that I had simply accepted as being a part of the country that I live in. But it was not only unusual buildings that he discovered; the Twat has an amazing knack of 'finding' things that I must have walked past a thousand times and never really noticed, such as murals, statues and hidden architecture.

In the summer of 2003, Brussels was decorated with life-size plastic cows that had been artistically painted and were part of an exhibition called *Art-on-Cows*. I believe that, previous to this, the exhibition had already taken place in several different countries using other cows, but this mad idea was exactly what was needed to tickle the Twat's fancy. Every boy likes to play, and this was right up the Twat's street. He would go out in the morning with his camera and try to spot as many different cows as possible and on various occasions he would meet somebody – usually an old man, which says a lot about the Twat, who was doing exactly the same thing. They would wander around the streets of Brussels together, with the Twat talking away in his very broken French, and give each other pointers as to other locations of cows. I believe that Quarsan ended up photographing over one hundred cows, and then, when they were finally auctioned off, he tried to persuade me to buy one to put in the front garden.

There are garden gnomes, there are life-size plastic cows. And then there are twats. When faced with a doe-eyed partner begging you to buy a life-size plastic cow that is being auctioned off for several thousand euros simply to put in the front garden, you have to treat him as you would a child by bringing him back to earth with a very firm "*No*". Men are very similar to children in many ways, especially when they want something, so be strong and hold your ground.

The Twat has also taken a strange liking to really, really appalling art. There are several shops in Brussels that sell some of the worst oil paintings imaginable, mainly pictures of landscapes, flowers and the like, and these shops hold an immense fascination for the Twat. Rather than pass by a shop selling these God-awful paintings, Quarsan just has to have a look and, if possible, take a photograph of the artwork in the shop window, much to his amusement. I truly believe that the man can find happiness wherever he is, as he manages to turn the most ghastly of monuments, art and culture into something really quite funny, even if it is only he who is laughing. So girls, it is always worth remembering that as long as your partner is happy, you'll at least get a bit of peace and quiet.

I refuse to let the man complain about this country now, as he keeps finding new things to do. He goes to concerts or shows that would never take place in England, he enjoys absurd artwork and crazy architecture, he is able to visit five different countries in one day without having to change currency, and so much more. Should your partner start complaining about where you live, then, before booking him on the next plane home, challenge him as to what, exactly, he has done, seen or even been involved in, in your homeland. If he remains negative about everything, book him an e-ticket back home and sweetly deliver the bill to him, along with his favourite supper into which you have spat several times and a glass of his favourite red wine that has been open for three days and has turned, like your thoughts about him, into pure vinegar.

MEETING THE KIDS

When Quarsan first joined our family, it was no secret that I had some excess baggage, notably twin daughters and a son. At first, the children were naturally wary of this strange man who had moved in with us, especially as they didn't understand much of what he was saying due to his northern accent and the fact that he muffled his words when he spoke (and still does). Still, he soon settled in and the children accepted him as part of the family, rather like a pet dog. Especially my son, who found that having another bloke around the house was just what he needed.

I should make it very clear here that the Twat is *not* the father of any of my children, despite a 'scare' about two years ago, and that I 'share' my children on an every-other-week basis with my ex-husband following an amicable, should there be such a thing, divorce.

The Twat would often take pity on my son and take him out for a hamburger. It soon became clear that he wasn't just being kind to my son. Oh no. Their excursions provided him with an excuse to get out of the house, grab a burger and escape from the female influence in our home. After the first time the Twat took my son out, I asked Jake what they'd spoken about and was told that he couldn't tell me as it was 'guy stuff'.

This 'guy stuff' stretched to the whereabouts of both my son and the Twat every weekday at 7pm. Downstairs, watching *The Simpsons*, but we females couldn't watch as it was 'guy stuff'. The two of them bonded very quickly and only fall out when Jake is asked to do anything.

It's not as if Quarsan has never met a child, he has – but he's never lived with one, so the bonding was quite a surprise. I often find that the Twat will gang up with the kids against me if I'm being unreasonable in their eyes, and the Twat is always the peace-keeper in the home, whether or not I happen to agree with him. I think my son brings out the child in Quarsan; not a difficult thing to do, as the two of them together are a lethal cocktail.

When the kids were younger, they would often be left in the hands of the Twat during the holidays whilst I went off to earn a few euros to buy some bread and, on a good day, butter as well. My partner would spend the entire morning in front of my computer, leaving the children to fend for themselves at lunchtime. He wouldn't join them for lunch, something that made me very angry as we were supposed to be a family, despite the fact that I couldn't be there as I was at the office. We finally had words and I told him that he was to eat with the children. It's the done thing.

Some days I'd leave Quarsan a note listing things that had to be done; not that I had much hope of him doing anything other than muck around on the internet. In the earlier days, I recall leaving Jake, who happened to have a nasty cough, in the hands of the Twat. As we were out of cough syrup, I asked the Twat if he'd buy some more and left the money on the table. This was obviously a bit much for him, for when I came home I asked Jake, who was jumping up and down on the sofa with the boy from next door, if the Twat had, indeed, bought some more cough mixture. The answer was negative but I wasn't to worry because "Your boyfriend gave me some of his". The Twat had a lot to learn, it appeared.

However, it did take a long time before the Quarsan would actually ask the kids to do anything himself. For example, we would all be working together clearing up the garden and he would forever be asking me to tell the kids what to do, when he was quite capable of delegating tasks amongst the three of them.

We would have frequent conversations along the lines of:

"Well, you give the orders then, smarty-pants."

"No, they're your kids."

"You live here, too and are their minder in the absence of their father."

"Look, I simply don't want them hosing down the front –"

"Then tell them that!"

It took the man three years before he could actually summon up the guts to ask my children to do something. Even now, he'd rather do the task himself than ask them to help, which, to my mind, defeats the purpose of having children, as I was always of the opinion that they were produced solely for slave labour and providing presents on my birthday, on Mothering Sunday and at Christmas.

Naturally, whenever something goes missing or the house is a tip, it is 100% my children's fault, regardless of what is missing and which part of the house looks a tip. Therefore it is *my* fault, and hence *my* duty, to get the children to sort it all out, even if the crisis in question has taken place in either my or the children's absence – i.e. when the Twat alone was in residence. It's called 'passing the blame on to someone else'.

As I mentioned earlier, the Twat bonded so well with my son, it was worrying. From the first day that he arrived in our household, the Twat did his very best to get on with my kids. He would pick up Jake from school during the winter months as I'd had a rather big falling out with one of the teachers. (This wasn't entirely my fault, as the teacher in question had run off with my ex-husband – before we were divorced.)

The Twat and my son even made biscuits together once (and they weren't called rock biscuits for nothing) and all in all, the two males in the house were the best of buddies. When driving back from school, the Twat would let my son sit on his lap and steer the car along the road up to our house where, it has to be said, Jake started 'parking' it perfectly straight alongside the front garden.

The pair of them obviously talked a lot about me as well. I learned about this when the Twat told me in all innocence one day that, "Your son can imitate you so well when you're angry". I shudder to think what else they did together, but it wasn't long before my son was referring to Quarsan as his 'quasi-papa', which I thought was rather sweet.

My daughters, on the other hand, have always been rather shy and it took them a while to come forward and actually ask Quarsan something. It usually went along the lines of, "Can he drive us to the skating-rink?" (for example), to which my reply would always be, "Of course he *can*, but I don't know if he *will* – so why don't you ask him yourselves?"

Quarsan tried very hard to gain the girls' confidence and he was often of more use than I when it came to homework, especially Biology which would involve a French dictionary, the *babelfish* translation website and the internet. He's also better at Maths, History and Geography than I am, so the girls often ask the Twat for help in those domains, leaving me to feel really quite useless as a parent.

My son isn't quite as friendly towards the Twat these days. Puberty hit the lad earlier than foreseen and now, on a bad day, Jake is as moody as a goth who has just been given a sunbed. If he can't get what he wants, then all hell breaks loose and, to be honest, the scene is not a pretty one. But seeing as the Twat knows quite a bit about computers, he is forever being badgered to download music (which I try my utmost to show my children is wrong, thus showing that I have *some* morals), and setting up internet games for Jake to play on. In fact, my son's favourite 'find' at the moment is *YouTube*, something that he spends hours watching – as does the man he admires: the Twat, the source of immense knowledge and the guy who knows all the scariest films that my son should watch.

The obsession with scary films would be worrying, but my children appear to be fairly sound, despite the films that Quarsan advises them to watch when asked for a scary DVD. The Twat went so far as to recommend *The Shining,* but my son didn't manage to watch it, as he was scared witless.

The Twat also has a theory that you can't be a proper bloke until you know about Michael Caine films, in particular *The Italian Job*, *The Ipcress File* and *Alfie*. When I stated that my son (at the time) was only 12, I was duly informed that they were the formative years and therefore very important. Following on from Michael Caine were the *Pink Panther* films and, naturally, James Bond. Jake also took to watching Austin Powers and both he and the Twat would go around either imitating Austin Powers or coming out with lines from the Bond films. At first, this was very funny. Now it gets on my tits.

So he's not totally useless after all.

If your partner is new to children and you just happen to have the odd child, then it is wise to make it clear who wears the trousers in the household. You do. You will find that your partner's childish tendencies come

out every now and then, but it is essential that if your offspring and your boyfriend misbehave, then they will all go to bed early without any supper, leaving you in the living room in perfect peace, doing just as you want. The introduction between your partner and your children should be done slowly for fear of frightening your child/children for life, as a twat is quite a lot to take on when you are only knee-high to a grasshopper. Obviously, a lot depends on the age of your children, but if they have reached the age of comprehension, you must, on all accounts, explain that the new man in the house is not the local plumber and nor is he the milkman, whatever his profession may be: he is a new member of the family. This means that, given a while, treating him like dirt is quite acceptable.

MEETING THE PARENTS

I have to admit to being very fortunate in that I have no in-laws, *per se*. My children's grandparents are always hovering in the background, but they are fairly easy to get on with if they know what's good for them and we have a good relationship still. In fact, I reckon it's probably better than when I was married, in which case I am all for divorce, though not the expenses that are involved. My ex-husband and I get on better than ever. I even speak to my sister-in-law – and never saw my brother-in-law anyway, so nothing has really changed there.

Quarsan, however, has no parents or grandparents still alive, and although I would have loved to have met them when they were still warm, I feel rather lucky not to have to go through the whole 'Meeting of the Parents' ritual again. He, on the other hand, has had to go through this after four years together. It was really rather difficult to get out of, seeing that my parents had very kindly paid for the journey to spend New Year's Eve with them somewhere in the South of England, not only for the children, but for the Twat and me as well.

I fell out with my parents several years before the Twat came along. It took him a long time to understand why I called them 'the Aliens' and why I didn't really want any contact with them at all. Being a parent myself has made me realise what children really need, regardless of their age. Support, love and understanding are only three factors, but they are incredibly important ones. I know I'm not the only one in this predicament – I know of some people who haven't spoken to their (living, not dead) parents for over ten years – but it's difficult trying to explain to someone else just how much not only I, but also my children, have been hurt by things my parents have said and done. I did think of the Aliens from time to time, but never for long. Having lived abroad for over twenty years has made me feel very excluded from the rest of the family. I have tried to mingle with them when we have met up in the past, I have invited them to stay whenever they want – as if your family *needs* to be invited, which mine does, apparently – but not once has any one of my three brothers stayed with me, let alone visited.

When Quarsan learnt of this news and saw that I did, in fact, want to visit them, he agreed to come along too, which was where the grooming started. I don't think that he is used to the company of people like my parents, and that New Year was horribly tense – probably because my mother was over-stressed and very tired. Beforehand, I tried teaching the Twat how to eat slowly, participate in the ongoing conversation rather than wolf down his food, and certainly not to burp or fart. He seemed to agree with these rather reasonable requests, but came back rather sharply when I told him that on no account was he to snore loudly.

The conversation went something like this…

"Listen, Zoe, you're going to have to learn not to shout and swear at me when we're at your parents."

"And you're going to have to learn how to eat slowly."

"I will. Like an ickle hamster."

"And you can't snore either."

"Well, I'm not going to sleep with them. Good Lord, woman, I have to draw the line somewhere."

And on that note, all five of us went to visit my parents, thanks to a lot of guidance from Quarsan as we embraced the London Underground, and a few major corrections as to which line to take from Waterloo to Paddington from the girls and I. My son followed on regardless, probably thinking that he was in France or somewhere, as he kept asking if we were 'under the sea yet'.

The trip down to the South of England was fine, until we reached a certain station that kept us delayed for 50 minutes. Then the stop before our final destination was also delayed, by which time the Twat was doing the inevitable on a packed train of commuters: snoring. Very loudly. No matter how many times I hit the poor man, he would simply snuffle, turn over and carry on, until at last I had to persuade him to wake up as we were 'nearly there'.

After a grunt, a bit of swearing and a glare at my children and me, we managed to get Quarsan, who was the strongest one amongst us, to help us all with our suitcases. We met the Parents, and this is when I really wanted to kick the Twat because he didn't exchange the pleasantries that had been so well drummed into me as a child when meeting 'new people', but, upon introduction, totally missed out on saying 'Mr' and 'Mrs'. Instead, he was warm, friendly and introduced himself without mentioning my parents' names at all. As a stickler for protocol and manners, this left me positively writhing in embarrassment as Hazel and Amber joined me to drive to the house in my mother's car, and the Twat and Jake went ahead in my father's car.

The Twat

At my parents' house, the Twat was introduced to one of my brothers, his wife and their two daughters, one of whom I'd not even seen yet, leaving me with only two more nieces to meet. However, being the sort of family we are, and having been raised in boarding schools apart from each other, we aren't particularly close. It's a bit like the Twat and his two nephews. When I ask him how old they are, his reply is something along the lines of, "This high". I think they may well be approaching the age of 20 – or more, by now – but they still remain "this high". Details have never really mattered to him.

We all managed to get along well during the ten days that we were there. On New Year's Eve we got kicked out to go for a walk as my parents had decided to cook a traditional Christmas dinner for the children, seeing as they hadn't had one that year. My father gave Quarsan a map and details of one of the walks and the children and I faithfully traipsed after the one person who knew exactly where he was going.

Or so we thought...

We managed to cross the same bridge four times, which was rich, seeing as our guide was a) a mountain climber and therefore was used to navigating his way around, and b) prided his navigation skills, especially as I, being a woman, am crap at it. We got caught in several very heavy downpours as we walked along a pathway made bumpy by rocks and tree roots. I was wet, cold and my back was positively killing me and, to top it all, the children wouldn't stop moaning at me … and then I sighted a pub. Oh joy! As we sat huddled around a roaring fire trying to dry off our clothes before we had to leave again, I knocked back a vodka and lime to temporarily numb the pain in my back whilst everybody else was drinking hot chocolate. Well, it was 10.30 in the morning.

When we found the telephone box that my father had mentioned, the Twat went in to give him a call to come and pick us up as planned. Cuddling up against each other like four penguins, the children and I waited outside in yet another downpour for my father to turn up while the Twat appeared to be waiting in the only dry place in the vicinity: the phone box. Finally, he came out and announced that he'd found the longer route and had asked my father if he would meet us at the end of that. Furious, and with no other option, we all carried on, weighed down by the mud that was clinging to our jeans right up to our knees and completely covering our hiking boots.

Once back at the house, we all had a hot bath each, then I attended to the children's blistered feet and knocked back a couple of painkillers. I don't believe that either the children or I said anything to the Twat until just after midnight, when whispers of "Happy New Year" were passed around after a wonderful Christmas dinner that involved the carving of possibly the largest turkey I have ever seen. The downside to buying an enormous turkey means, of course, that over the course of the following week you will be eating turkey sandwiches, turkey stew, fried turkey, grilled turkey and even turkey curry.

Needless to say, we were sent home on our long train journey back with turkey sandwiches, lovingly made by my mother. Even the Twat had had enough by this time, and not many were eaten...

I believe that the Twat made a good impression on my parents since they visited us twice during the following year and so all those nerves and extra worry lines were for nothing. I obviously can let him out of the house – on a good day.

The first time that you introduce your partner to your parents is always the worst, especially if your parents and your loved one come from extremely different backgrounds. But remember, opposites can, and very often do, attract, which can be a good thing. It can also be a Bad Thing in that they get on so well together that should you be visiting for a period of time, the likelihood of seeing your partner is slim, and you may well find yourself spending more time with the household pets than anyone else.

It is extremely important to strike an even balance and ensure that there are things that you and your partner would like to do together. This is for two reasons: a) your parents may take a strong dislike to your partner; or b) they may take him under their wing and discuss all those topics that bore you to death, such as the latest cricket test or Schumacher's performance at the Grand Prix last week. So, for the sake of your own sanity, do prepare some outings together, without your parents.

But at the risk of your partner trashing your mum's car,

I really would advise going somewhere local, such as a quiet, homely pub, as this will avoid having to borrow your mum's car to get out and about in, especially if it's an automatic car, something that your loved one may never have driven before.

The Twat
at Home

SLEEPING WITH A TWAT

Before deciding to sleep with a twat, it is always advisable to be prepared. You should make sure that you have good ear plugs, air freshener, your own pillow and duvet and, in extreme cases, your own mattress, and a good, hard slipper. Even a spare room can come in handy.

Experience has taught me that most men tend to suffer badly from flatulence, which can not only be incredibly pungent but is often expelled from the body so noisily that even I have been woken up in the middle of the night during one of my boyfriend's long and loud farts. This is surprising, as very little wakes me up during the night and it is only on very rare occasions that the DHL flights landing at the airport not far from where we live manage to wake me, by sounding as if they are landing in the bedroom. But when I say that sharing a bed with the Twat is like sleeping with someone who has a trumpet stuck up their arse, I couldn't be closer to the truth.

Then there is the other problem: snoring. Having been kept awake night after night by my boyfriend's snoring, I decided to invest in several pairs of heavy-duty ear plugs. These work to an extent, but they never quite drown out the sound of his heavy breathing. In and out it goes, followed by constant coughing and wheezing, and there is only so much pushing and shoving that I can do before a swift, but hard, kick in the shins is the only way to shut him up. You will not in any way be appreciated for this rather violent act, but you may finally get some peace and quiet, and if you dislike the idea of kicking your boyfriend in the shins, then use the slipper.

Some men tend to move around during the night, often taking over the entire bed, no matter how big yours may be. This will mean that you will probably lose all possession of your pillow and may well find yourself on the brink of falling out of bed. I have learnt the fine art of rolling over my boyfriend and taking up his side of the bed, although this does come with a caution: be careful that he doesn't roll back and flatten you in the process. There is nothing worse than waking up to the feeling of several crushed ribs.

If all of this sounds like too much hard work, use the spare mattress – or the spare bed.

There are other problems too, such as sleep-talking. Although the Twat doesn't sleep-talk that much, he can make a terrible racket sometimes. There was one time when I was woken up by the entire mattress moving as the Twat was laughing away like a hyena. The noise was awful and as soon as he dozed off again, he started laughing again until I ended up hitting him and telling him to shut up. Apparently, I sleep-talk, and very often in French. Because the Twat doesn't understand French, there has been many an occasion when he has joined in the conversation, starting off by asking me to switch to English as he can't follow what I'm on about. The strangest bit is the fact that I *do* switch to English and start having conversations of which I am completely unaware until the next morning, when the Twat will tell me all about it.

Sleeping with a twat is akin to sleeping with a hippopotamus who snores, growls and farts throughout the night. Think about the options: once the horizontal jogging is over and done with, either you or your partner could move to a completely different room for a decent night's sleep – or you could simply put up with the noise and never, ever complain about the sleepless nights again.

But there again, if your partner is into BDSM (Bondage, Domination, Sado-masochism) and enjoys being punched, kicked or slapped senseless with a hard slipper, that really is a matter that should be kept between the two of you.

SHOPPING WITH A TWAT

The idea of going shopping with an extra pair of arms is always an appealing one, until the day you realise that your boyfriend has a memory like a sieve. The first few times I went to the supermarket with Quarsan, I'd give him a long shopping list to hold onto whilst I was putting my shoes on. Once we got inside the supermarket, the Twat would then ask me, without fail, where the shopping list was, to which I'd reply that he had it and he, in turn, would inform me that no, he didn't, he put it on the kitchen table.

The frustration and anger that I used to feel once it occurred to me that my boyfriend was not only a twat, but also a complete and utterly useless waste of space, has no bounds. But I never took it out on him as he was there, helping me do the shopping, and for that I was grateful. Trying to shop for five people from memory has resulted in several trips back to the supermarket to get certain items that were on the missing shopping list – which, of course, tested an awful lot of patience.

I don't like shopping for clothes, but I thoroughly enjoy grocery shopping as I like to check out any new food item that has been introduced into our little corner of the world. The Twat, on the other hand, has absolutely no time at all for this. A week's load of shopping can be done by him in half an hour, compared to my leisurely stroll around the aisles, looking at different condiments and the like. This annoys the Twat no end, especially as one minute we're standing next to each other and the next, he'll find himself running around the super-market on the point of yelling out my name as I appear to have 'vanished'. I can't help myself, I am simply interested in what's available to eat and love the idea of buying something different that will introduce a change into our usual diet.

As a result of this, my dearest kindly asked me if I'd stop going shopping with him as he can do it so much faster. I really do admire Quarsan's fast shopping skills – I'm rather like that when shopping for clothes – but therein lies another problem…

He may have shot around the supermarket like Speedy Gonzales on crack, but he forgets to buy necessary items. Such as fruit. Toilet and/or, kitchen paper. Tissues. Toothpaste, and possibly the Twat's favourite forgettable item – vegetables. Even when holding a shopping list in his hand, the idiot will still forget to buy necessary items and I'd be lying if I said that it doesn't annoy me – especially when he returns home with tubs of hummus that I have paid for, then scoffs the entire lot. He does this quite often – eats my fridge clean. Apart from vegetables, that is.

I remember one occasion when I had bought some fairly expensive smoked ham as a treat for the two of us. One evening, when Quarsan was out learning French at his 'Belgian class', so-called as Quarsan finds it hilarious that a country as small as Belgium has three official languages, I fancied making myself a small salad, including a couple of pieces of the ham I had bought. I looked for it everywhere, but couldn't find it. When he got home, I asked him if he had put it somewhere else and his reply was, "Oh yes, I ate it".

When your partner offers to get the shopping in for you, whatever it may be, unless you happen to be living with a near-perfect man, just say 'no', for more reasons than one.

When my toaster decided to cark it and meet its maker in toaster Heaven, I was set on replacing the old one with an identical model. My boyfriend offered to go and replace the dead toaster whilst I sat outside the shop in the car. When taking him up on his kind offer, I'd reminded him that it had to be chrome; a matt, chrome toaster. He came out with a white, plastic toaster and he is still, to this day, trying to justify himself by saying that it does have a bit of chrome on it, and then went on to detail the many useless features that assisted his decision to buy it.

If your partner insists on accompanying you to the supermarket, take it as a compliment, but make sure that you have the shopping list ready in your pocket and, to be ultra-efficient, take a biro as well so as to tick off the items bought. Should your beloved then insist on going shopping alone 'as it's quicker', then make sure that he has a list, a biro and, if possible, a child to accompany him and remind him of the items that need buying. Be strict. If your partner forgets something vital, then send him back to get it, and if he buys something that is totally unnecessary and more of a luxury, then it's time to switch roles and do the shopping yourself. Or make him pay for everything. It's a well-known fact that twats will never get what you actually want, especially when it comes down to groceries, as their ideal, in general, is a ready-made meal and damn any fresh vegetables.

Having a twat accompany you when you have to buy an article of clothing or two, normally takes a lot of persuasion from your side, especially if you dislike shopping for clothes yourself. Personally, I like to have someone with me to give me a second opinion about the outfits I'm trying on. When it comes to the Twat, though, the most I ever get out of him by way of opinion is a grunt, which is hardly surprising coming from someone who describes a bra as 'boobie buckets' and asks why I can't make do with two shopping bags and some string instead. Most of the time, I'll find the Twat sitting outside the shop reading a book while trying to sneak in a cigarette, which isn't that helpful at all. Although he did once have the audacity to ask me why I'd bought a pair of sandals when I said I was going to buy a pair of *shoes*. I thought this was a bit much, especially after the ordeal with the toaster.

Commonsense dictates that if you don't have teenage daughters, then take a female friend with you. Men are useless at dishing out advice when it comes to clothes-shopping; yes, your arse *will* look big in that, but he will say the contrary. Yes, that *is* 'your' colour and it suits you magnificently, despite it clashing with the colour of your hair. And those trousers *will* look great on you despite the fit being so tight that you are sporting the World's Largest Camel Toe.

And be warned: if they are buying clothes for themselves, your opinion is the very last thing they want.

Another common trait in possibly all men is that they simply Will Not Ask For Help, be it directions, or whether the shop that you are standing in stocks whatever you are looking for. The Twat would rather dither around a shop for hours looking for something, rather than ask an all-too-eager salesman for help, whereas I will simply ask and get an answer, whether it is positive or negative. This is probably why the Twat hates IKEA so much.

I know of a lot of people who hate IKEA, but the Twat hates it to the extent that, even when bribed to go there, he'll do it only on the condition that he can yank me around the shop by my thumb and only buy exactly what I need. So when we needed a CD rack, that is exactly what we left with. When we needed a garden parasol and didn't like any of the ones they had in stock, we left empty-handed. I almost feel bullied when going around the displays in that enormous warehouse of a shop that gives the most ridiculous names to each item it sells – but when I want to go to IKEA, I need a driver, and the Twat is the only one of us who can drive.

The last time we went there, we borrowed a friend's car that was too small to fit yet another CD rack into, but just large enough to contain the lights that we so badly needed for the hallway of the house. On this occasion, the only way I managed to bribe Quarsan to go into the place was by promising to buy him lunch at the cafeteria, food being the obvious way to a man's heart. Although the food was very good, the cafeteria was full of stressed mothers with screaming children and the noise factor was very, very loud. As the IKEA nearest to us is in the middle of an industrial state, their cafeteria also appears to cater for all the big office blocks nearby, and so the very idea of a quiet lunch there is out of the question, and didn't help the Twat's mood.

The secret to men and shopping is a fairly simple solution: give them the internet, where they can spend weeks bidding for useless and unnecessary items on eBay with their own money. How many more inflatable Daleks do we need?

EATING WITH A TWAT

The Twat will eat just about anything apart from eggs, which is just as well, given his history of excessive flatulence. Although his manners aren't that bad, they aren't that good, either. But perhaps the most amazing thing about the Twat is the speed at which he can, and does, eat. I often wonder if he even tastes the food, although he must do, as he very much appreciates what gets served at the cheap little Italian restaurant near the office.

I find that I barely have time even to pick up my fork and there is Quarsan, sitting opposite me, already finished. His food must barely touch his tongue. Like a dog eating a treat, it gets swallowed straight down as he shovels in his next forkful. He doesn't talk during a meal, nor does he put down his knife and fork. He simply eats, non-stop, sometimes pausing for a sip of wine, but his concentration is entirely on his food. Dried sauce-drips can often be found splattered on his T-shirts, which he doesn't change for days, making it quite easy for the world to see exactly what he has been eating over the past week. This causes a problem in that frequently, by the time his tops make it to the washing machine, the stains are there to stay.

In his former life, back in Cumbria, food had always been considered merely as fuel to get the Twat up the mountains, not something to actually enjoy. That was a concept of which he was completely unaware. Besides, British cuisine, although getting better, has never been known as something to savour. Arriving in Belgium where the food can be just as good as in France, and learning to actually enjoy what he is eating, has been a bit of a learning curve for the Twat.

The huge downside to his newly-acquired love of food is that, given the chance, he'll eat me out of house and pocket without even thinking about what he's done. On several occasions, when friends from the UK brought over Cheddar cheese for us, I never even got a sniff of it as the Twat had gobbled it up before it even made it to the fridge. This made me so angry that now I make sure I hide any gifts of Cheddar cheese I may receive. Not only does the Twat never offer to share out such delicious luxuries, he doesn't even care about whether or not I would like some, and he certainly doesn't seem to be conscious of his ever-expanding waistline. It drives me mad.

In 2006, my parents gave us a hamper full of the most wonderful goodies, including a Christmas pudding and a Christmas cake. I was considering using the cake as a doorstop as I really, really dislike Christmas cake – and Christmas pudding, too – but when I went downstairs to evaluate the damage that we had caused on Christmas day, I noticed that half the cake had already been eaten. Half of the untouched cheese had gone, too and, as usual, the hummus was but an empty tub of which I had had none.

This kind of behaviour tends to happen all the time. Only last week, I left half a pizza in the fridge, intending to finish it the following day. The next day, I mumbled something about getting out the remaining half of the pizza, to which the Twat replied, "It's not there. I ate it this morning". Thinking about it, it does anger me, but it happens so often that there's no point in making a fuss – I'll just make an omelette for dinner the following day. He's allergic to eggs.

Although Quarsan acts as a human vacuum cleaner and will finish up any food that the kids don't want, his waste-disposal habit isn't all that helpful to me, really, because I am trying to bring the children up to eat everything on their plates. Another problem is that, as he is the person who does all the cooking (relieving me of a chore that I have come to hate), it means that there are never any vegetables – apart from potatoes – or fruit in the house. They are 'too healthy', according to the Twat, and so I often nip down to the super-market with Hazel to buy fruit and a lettuce or two. This rather selective eating may well derive from the fact that the Twat lived with the Maasai for a while and believes that the only food you need is meat. He survived living in Tanzania for four months eating only meat.

Should you live with someone who eats as fast as my boyfriend does, then don't even bother spending your precious time cooking up delicious meals with the aim of getting to your partner's heart because he won't taste a thing. A quick meal slung together here and there will earn you as many brownie points as a three-course meal lovingly assembled at great expense.

So why bother?

If your partner tends to eat you out of house and home, then make sure that there is only enough food in the fridge for that night's supper. If he goes as far as eating not only his share but yours, too, then take yourself out for a good meal – using his credit card. You can't say that you didn't enjoy a good meal after all of that, can you?

TAKING OVER THE HOUSE

When a twat moves in with you, he will want to make the house as much his as it is yours, and will do so without so much as asking, thus committing crimes against interior design all over the place. Expect complaints about your interior decorating, the pictures that you hang on the walls, your clutter, the fact that your bed faces north – and this is just the beginning. Imagine if your partner is moving in with you from a *different country altogether...*

THE SATELLITE DISH

One of the first discoveries that the Twat made after having moved in with us was the lack of television. Not the lack of a television *per se*, but the lack of English-speaking channels. I always thought that we were fairly lucky in that most of the Dutch channels would air a film or TV series in its original language, whereas the French channels would dub them into French, thus losing a lot of the humour. Spoilt with BBC1, BBC2 and News24, plus the Dutch channels for any English/American films/soaps, I was very happy. The Twat, on the other hand, was not. He was used to Channel 4 and all the other channels that you get in the UK and so grumbled for a while until he finally got used to it. With CNN and CNBC, the man got enough coverage of the goings-on in the world to amuse himself no end.

Until, that is, Flanders decided to go digital. Overnight, we were stripped of CNN, CNBC, News24 and several other French and even Belgian channels. Even I was pissed off by this stage, as News24 had a far better coverage than some of the other channels, and my daughters lost a French channel which showed their current American soap. In French. The whole idea behind going digital was for each household to buy a 'digibox' and if you wanted to record from the television set, then you had to buy a new DVD player. Mmmmm, a scam, perhaps? Quarsan begged for a 'digibox', I said no and no it remained, until I made friends with a reader of my site who just happened to live in this country and had found someone who was in ... you've guessed it ... the satellite business.

I had sworn blind that I would never have a big, ugly satellite dish on my house and it remained that way for years until, finally, the Twat made an appointment for the satellite man to visit the house. He was warned well in advance about my feelings towards satellite dishes and was well prepared for the visit. He went out into the garden and looked at the roof and, between the Twat and himself, convinced me that a dish could be put on my house 'ever so discreetly'. Stupidly, I let my guard down and Mr Satellite came round a week or two later to install the dish. Over a light lunch the Twat told me that there were, in fact, two dishes. *TWO?*

"Oh yes," I was told, "but the second one is a smaller one – for the children, as they so miss some of the French programmes that they no longer get."

Aha, the 'children' tactic. I was assured that it was 'ever so discreet', the picture on the television was much better now, as was the sound – and I'd love it.

We went home.

I looked at the roof and yelled for the criminal who had had the dishes installed to get his camera out and take photographic evidence of these 'discreet' satellite dishes. The larger one is almost twice the size of the smaller one and it was then that it was pointed out that it was the bigger one that was for the French channels. This made absolutely no sense whatsoever to me and so, furious, and not in the least bit interested in the television, I went to bed, not having been in the best of health over the previous couple of days, where I temporarily managed to blot out the Twat's latest crime by sleeping for a couple of hours.

My house had been vandalised by a complete and utter idiot who has absolutely no taste when it comes to exterior decorating. And yet, when I think of it, this may not be so much of an 'idiot thing' but a 'bloke thing', perpetrated by a typical bloke who clings onto somebody stupid enough to finally give way after several years of saying "no". It is wise to look out for such traits in your partner or else you may well find that your house suddenly starts looking like a spaceship.

THE SHED
The satellite dishes were only the latest in a series of additions that the Twat has made to my home. Perhaps I should point

out that it all started with a shed. The man wanted a shed desperately but, in all honesty, my garden isn't big enough to accommodate a shed so the answer to that was a straight "no". Sheds are very much a bloke thing, that bit I understand, but when you live with someone who has to bring the lack of a shed up at least once every week, it gets to be a little tiresome. And so the Twat started trying different approaches in the hope of softening me up. He told me he'd get a TV and a network connection in 'his' shed, as well as a coffee maker. Turning what should be a place to house your bicycles, lawn mower, garden furniture and gardening equipment into a second home, did not go down very well with me.

Once he realised that hadn't worked, he tried a different approach. He'd transform the shed into a wine bar so that I could go and enjoy a glass of wine and experiment with making different cocktails. For reasons that went straight above his bloke-ish head, that idea went down like a lead balloon, too. Girls, I feel sure you'll sympathise with me on this one. I like a drink in the comfort of my own home, or even out somewhere. But not in a shed.

His next idea was to install a bunk-bed, TV and a couple of

armchairs, so that he and Jake would have somewhere to escape 'once a month'. This suggestion went down the worst of the lot. I told him in no uncertain terms that when you live with three women, you have to put up with the way their bodies work as well. Readers of my website have sympathised with Quarsan and have even tried bullying me into allowing him to have a shed, but so far I have stood my ground and instead he gets sent an annual 'shed calendar' by one reader. A male, naturally.

THE GADGETS

If I go back a few years, I can see how the Twat has slowly transformed my home into a bloke's paradise, although I'm not sure all men or any women would put up with the things I have to endure on a daily basis. The Twat's sense of interior design is far from aesthetic, and as I walk around the house I keep finding things that I know I certainly didn't buy. My bedroom is better now, thanks to several trips down to the tip, but there are still two unused laptops by the side of my bed, neither of which belong to me, nor do they work. Then came the introduction of an MP3/CD/cassette player as a birthday present one year. This, said the Twat, was for me to have in my office at home to listen to music on whilst typing, as listening to CDs whilst bashing away on the keyboard wasn't always a great idea because the CDs would jump every time I hit 'enter'. That bulky machine soon vanished into the kitchen, never to return again, so that the Twat would have music to listen to while cooking.

When I mentioned the disappearance of my CD player, the Twat simply shrugged his shoulders and asked if I wanted feeding or not. The price I had to pay in return for a cook was not a big one, but it's strange how so many of the gifts that I have been given by my boyfriend have ended up in his possession. It is for this reason that I prefer to be given perfume, or something equally unsuitable for his tastes – or that I simply buy the items I need myself.

My house was obviously incomplete in his opinion as I didn't have a DVD player, so one day the Twat managed to install one. Although this was a good idea, the piece of hardware in question turned out to be a complete and utter eyesore, as the only way that it could be connected up to the television was by opening a flap at the front of the TV and sticking four wires into the respective sockets. As if this wasn't bad enough, the Twat went and bought a 'home cinema' from eBay which basically involved one large speaker that is currently underneath the table that the television is on, five 'mini speakers' that are dotted around the TV as far as humanly possible – and an awful lot of wires connecting the whole lot up. I am absolutely positive that there must be a better, more aesthetic way of obtaining great picture and sound quality than the present system, which makes my living room look as if it has more wires and cables in it than a neo-natal ward.

Another example of why I feel my house has been taken over by an alien is the sheer mess that Quarsan manages to make. As somebody who reads an incredible number of books and magazines, there are always piles of them everywhere, often spread around the living room and dining area and the loo floors are covered with copies of *Private Eye*. Then there is his music. We are desperately in need of a third CD rack as there are DVDs and CDs lying around everywhere, because the two CD racks that I already own are so full that there are even CDs piled on top of each of them. Considering that each rack holds 200 CDs, this shows there are quite a lot of the things. Probably in excess of 1,000. I mean, how many can you listen to in the average year, with only two ears?

It is a difficult dilemma to face: your boyfriend and his world, or no boyfriend at all.

THE JARS
What really gets my goat are empty jars. The first time that the Twat left here to go back to England for three weeks, to do a job on top of a mountain, I felt pretty miserable, especially when the kids were at their dad's. This house is far too big for one person, and so all the old feelings of being alone came back to haunt me. To pass the time, I would spend longer hours at the office and then pass the time at home doing bizarre things such as cleaning out the fridge, a chore that I abhor. As I emptied the fridge of all its jars, I was amazed at just how many were empty. Who on earth would put an empty jar back in the fridge? The children do not eat marmalade, curry paste, pickle sauces, mustard – in fact, they don't even put jars back in the fridge, full stop. The culprit was standing on the top of a mountain somewhere in Cumbria.

So I kept the evidence, ready to give the culprit a Spanish Inquisition upon his return. As soon as he was back, I forced the Twat to sit down and look at the empty jars that had been on the kitchen table for about a week.

Me: "Jar one from Exhibit A: chutney. Now, do tell me why this empty jar has been put back in the fridge."

The Guilty One, after examining the pot and opening it: "It's not mine."

Me: "I know that, but you did have some, you have eaten some, the children don't eat it, so it has to be you."

Guilty One: "Not mine."

Me: "Okay. Now jar number two: mango chutney. Can you explain to me... "

Guilty One: "Yes. I put it in the fridge 'cos I thought it was nice."

Me: "Nice? You returned an empty jar of mango chutney to the fridge because you thought it was nice?"

Guilty One: "Well, yeah, and so I could fill it up with water and add it to a Thai sauce and make it nicer 'cos it's nice and stuff."

Me: "And I suppose this applies to the chili pickle too? Don't answer, let's move on. You're a pathetic liar. These two jars – marmalade and jam. Make this a good explanation."

The Guilty One, peering into each of the empty jars, said: "There's enough in here to cover two slices of toast."

Me: "There isn't enough in there to feed a starving flea, let alone cover a piece of toast. Let's look at Exhibit B. I know what you're going to say about the bowl."

Guilty One: "The bowl? Dunno about that. Tell me, Sweetest."

Me: "When I opened the fridge to clean it I found this bowl in it – I presume that there was once salad in it but why did you put an empty, dirty bowl back into the fridge? And can you explain these empty jars of chocolate spread?"

Guilty One: "Oh yes, the bowl. Ummm, it had salad in it, I think. And the chocolate spread is not mine, it's your son's."

He then peered into the other empty chocolate spread jar and said, "Nope. That's your son's, too."

Me: "How strange. Jake rarely eats the stuff." (This has, however, dramatically changed since then.)

Guilty One: "It's his. 'Appen."

And that is only half the story of things that I find in the fridge that should otherwise be elsewhere, but it gives you an idea of the Twat's uniquely peculiar world.

The trick of involving your children, should you have any, is an old one and widely used to get whatever a man wants, even satellite dishes. I failed miserably at that test and relented, giving my boyfriend exactly what he wanted, plus an extra satellite dish *"for the children"*. There is only one channel that they watch from the eyesore that is now on my house, but I decided not to tell my boyfriend that; not after he had paid for the dishes and the installation. As I had given in too easily, I thought that perhaps I should be cruel to be kind, in a manner of speaking.

When your partner decides to transform your home into some sort of paradise of his own, it is time to start thinking of moving out and finding something together where you can start anew on common ground. A fresh start in a newly decorated home is the best way to begin a relationship as from there, you can mould into each other's way of living.

If your loved one is desperate for a garden shed, no matter how small your garden is, let him have one – just don't forget about bonfire night. If he insists on turning your living room into a scrap-heap of wires, just don't forget that wires can be removed and thrown out. And if your beloved keeps on replacing empty jars back into the fridge – then padlock it.

BEING 'HELPFUL'

TWAT IN THE GARDEN
The Twat has a way of making himself look as if he is genuinely being extremely helpful. Yet, at the same time, although he may actually *be* helpful, he has the most amazing ways of going about it. One of his specialities is gardening. Although it is a great relief to me that he should be kind enough to help me mow the lawn – if I do so much as plug the lawn mower

in I tend to injure my back – the Twat gets grumpy, takes over (anything, rather than have to put up with me and a bad back), and speeds around the lawn as fast as possible so as to get back to his computer.

The first time he mowed the lawn for me, I remember looking out of the bedroom window and noticing that, although the grass was shorter, only parts of it were. There were strips of long grass all over the lawn in the areas the Twat had completely missed. When I pointed this out to him, he casually mentioned that he was trying to turn the garden into a race track.

One summer, my dearest had gathered the children and myself together in order to tackle the garden. This involved cutting back a tree and various other activities that might come under the 'gardening' label. This seemed to be a good idea until I saw that he had borrowed a ladder, which was propped up against a tall, thin tree. With about 50 metres of his climbing rope and two mountaineering clips, he proceeded to climb up it. The Twat managed to attach the ladder to the tree by using the clips and then tried very hard to throw the rope up into the tree. After a lot of swearing, he came back down and tried throwing the rope up the tree from the ground. It was at this point that I thought it a good idea to ask him what on earth he was doing. Basically, the Twat planned to attach the rope around the tree and saw it off at a certain level, while I pulled the tree over via the rope which I was to attach around my waist.

I didn't like the idea of this one little bit. Amber and Jake had scarpered whilst Hazel stayed behind simply to take photos. This was, in fact, the worst bit of tree-pruning that I have ever witnessed in my life. I ended up with a very sore back but my boyfriend was happy – he'd cut back the tree by several metres, but his future as a tree surgeon is over for good. He did, however, make good use of the tree trunk that was lying in the middle of the garden. He stripped it of all its branches and used it as the top bar for Jakes's rather unusual, but totally natural, goal post.

The first time the Twat offered to help me tidy up around the pond, I was very happy at the prospect. The idea was to cut back the grass around my beloved pond and clear it of blanket weed. As I scooped out dead leaves, being careful not to throw out any newts – I have plenty and am passionate about them – the Twat was working at the other end, scooping out enormous amounts of weeds, dead leaves and any other foliage that had fallen into the water. I carried on doing my thing at my end, leaving the Twat to carry on with the excellent job he appeared to be doing. Heads bowed, we talked without looking at each other, until finally we decided to call it a day, and a damned good one too. We had both put in a lot of hard work to maintain my pond that afternoon, and had Quarsan not been around, I would have seriously buggered up my back – again.

As we stood up at last and admired our hard work, I suddenly realised that something was wrong ... and then it clicked.

"Where are my waterlily buds?" I asked Quarsan. They had been perfectly visible through the clear, newly cleansed water.

"Oh, those weeds? I pulled them all out."

I nearly cried and ever since that day, which was several years ago now, I have repeatedly asked for my waterlilies to be replaced, but as of yet, no such luck. It has also resulted in a big drop in the numbers of dragonflies that stay around the pond. All round, it was quite a tragedy and something which only a true twat could possibly pull off.

Men either love or hate gardening, and those in the latter group look upon it as a time to flex those muscles, show them off and then sit down for a pint. The flowery bits of the garden are for girls, obviously, which, if alright by you, is just fine. But those of the opposite sex who simply adore gardening will put you through sheer hell, as everything that *you* do Will Be Wrong. You will prune the roses a millimetre too short, miss out on the one piece of clover still left on your immaculate, weed-free lawn and fail to trim the borders to his satisfaction. If you end up with a partner who appears to love his garden more than you, then get out the chaise longue, a good book and relax under a shady tree while he toils away. After all, there is no need for two to suffer, is there?

TWAT ABOUT THE HOUSE

After a late night when I decided to collapse into bed in the early hours of the morning because I couldn't stand the sound of the Twat puffing on a cigarette and coughing away outside anymore, I woke up feeling fairly dynamic. This is unusual for me, especially on a Sunday morning and being very much a 'bed person'. I had to do something and if I didn't do it that very day, it would haunt me for the rest of my days to come. The chore I had planned was The Annual Cleaning-Out of The Fridge.

My God, there was no stopping me as I leapt out of bed, threw on my huge tracksuit, brushed my teeth and marched into the kitchen before Quarsan even had time to make me a cuppa. That's how dynamic I was feeling. So powered-up, in fact, that I threw the man completely off balance as he's not quite used to so much energy emanating from me at that time in the morning. All he wanted to do was stay in the living room watching Frost on the television whilst minding his own business. But no, he couldn't do that because I was cleaning out the fridge and so he had to offer to help because: "You've got a bad back and your arm hurts."

This was very sweet of the Twat and I appreciated it, especially as I was recovering from an accident that I'd had a few weeks earlier. I had slipped over on a sloping pathway and, for fear of hurting my back, I had grabbed onto the fence while my body kept sliding downwards. This resulted in my straining all my arm muscles as I kept tight hold of the fence, which wasn't a clever thing to do. Still, it earned me some sympathy votes and help with a chore that I very much dislike doing... Or should I rephrase that and put 'an offer of help', as the Twat was about as helpful as a twat could be.

That day, the Twat happened to be suffering from a heavy cold. He stood there wheezing and snorting back rivers of snot until I asked him to please blow his nose – at which he snapped back at me and finally grabbed a tissue. I hate people who sniff, I really do. I mean, whatever happened to manners?

As the pots leapt out of The Fridge at me for their annual bath, leaving behind a very murky interior festooned with multi-coloured stains, some of which were actually moving, the old man groaned and asked if we really had to empty The Fridge before cleaning it.

My boyfriend did everything in his power to get the job over and done with as quickly as possible, which was, in all honesty, my aim, too, except that I had some snivelling old git moaning and sniffling and whining away, making the whole job even worse than it already was. Then he decided to take over. He took out all the shelves and I gave them a thorough scrub-down down while he wiped the pots.

Then it was time to see what was still lurking within. I wasn't surprised to find a huge, empty jar of Marmite, onions that were growing legs, limp bits of ginger, rancid butter, several tomatoes that had grown an extra white, fuzzy skin and other unidentifiable oddities that ended up in the bin.

Quarsan stood back to allow me room to attack the interior of The Fridge, which entailed dodging certain dangerous-looking blobs splattered all over the surfaces, notably on the bottom. I felt as if I were entering a zone where Weapons of Mass Deterioration were hidden, and I wondered whether there was any need for a gas-mask. Once it was all scrubbed down, with the help of the Twat's eyes and hands on my backside and nothing more, I felt it safe to put things back into The Fridge. This is where the Twat was his most helpful, passing me, in between sniffs, all the half-wiped jars as I re-arranged them around the spotless Fridge.

I think most people will agree that two pairs of hands are better than one. So if your partner offers to help you with a certain chore, then stop complaining, woman, and accept. But when he stands there moaning and sniffling with a bad cold, yet still insisting on helping rather than going back to bed, it can make life awkward. The answer is to make the job look as unpleasant as possible and martyr yourself into doing it alone by heavy sighing and the odd, "Oh, I'll cope, despite the pain", so that your partner will end up going back to bed – possibly feeling worse than before. There is nothing better than the sensation of having achieved a small victory.

TWAT IN THE KITCHEN

One day, I had had enough and told the children and the Twat that I'd given up cooking and that, from then on, if they wanted something to eat, one of them would have to cook it. I don't know why I suddenly disliked cooking, especially after having just bought a rather good wok-cookbook with the simplest of recipes, but I had. The kitchen is nothing more than a fleeting memory to me now. I only use it as a route to get to my stash of red wine in the garage or, if I can be bothered, in the cellar. I am a lazy woman, but then lazy women don't end up writing books so I must be doing something right.

The first time I announced that I was about to give up cooking, I decided to go about it the sly way. My daughters were then 15 years old which, in my books, means that they should already be bringing a healthy income into the household, but there's this damn thing called 'school' that gets in the way. So, I told Amber and Hazel that I wasn't cooking that weekend and that they had better see to it. After several hearty debates as to what they should cook, I suggested something that they liked, my daughters agreed to it and I gave them the money to go out and buy the ingredients.

"But what? How much? Not *real* mashed potato, please?"

I gave in to their desire for 'fake mash', but I have to admit that the meal that they prepared was very good indeed.

After that, Quarsan took over and he isn't a bad cook, thanks to jars of ready-made curry sauces and the never-ending meals of fresh pasta, lasagne, moussaka and the like that he churns out. After a week of ready-made lasagne, pizzas and tortellini with a sauce out of a jar, the children got fed up and so he had to experiment. He managed to fish out my wok and has used it to death ever since, and I could eat his Thai 'stir-fries' for every meal. Unfortunately for me, though, one of my daughters has a hatred of anything healthy, especially vegetables, so now I can only enjoy a stir-fry when the children are with their father for a week.

Quarsan regularly turns out favourites such as 'pasta-bakes', chicken korma, 'wraps' and other such delicacies that children like. As long as there are no vegetables visible, the entire lot gets eaten, and I very much appreciate him for cooking not only for the two of us, when the children aren't around, but for the whole family.

There is always a 'but' to good deeds such as these and this is probably the most painful one of all: why does he have to leave the kitchen in such a state? The cooker always needs a good cleaning after the Twat has attacked the kitchen, as does literally every single surface. At first, I used to pace behind him, putting away condiments, herbs and the like, the moment he had finished using them, only to have him shout at me because he couldn't find things. So now I leave him in peace to be as messy as he likes, and I come downstairs to the kitchen afterwards to clean all the surfaces and the sinks, and finally rinse the cloths and hang up the soaking wet tea towels. I even know how to find him simply by following the little, sticky coffee stains he leaves behind him on the tiles, whenever he makes himself a cup of coffee and takes it either to the living room, or upstairs.

There is help and there is help.

The Twat finds it immensely amusing when he leaves for a week or two to visit friends in England and stop off to do some conservation work, as it means that there will be an entire period when I will have to cook for the kids and myself. The last time this happened, Amber received a text message from him which read: *DO NOT LET YOUR MOTHER INTO THE KITCHEN*. But the last laugh was on him as I had organised a rota whereby we would each cook a meal a day and, due to the children not being around on a couple of those days, I only ended up cooking twice. Even better, as the children have been brought up to clean after themselves as they cook, unlike the Twat. The kitchen was spotless, too.

Quarsan may be proud of his culinary skills, but he has obviously forgotten the time I asked him to bake me a birthday cake…

I bought a cake-mix for him, gave him the packet, the front of which boasted a beautiful chocolate cake, and more or less ordered the Twat to make the cake. On seeing the cake on the packet, his eyes lit up in agreement, but of course, cakes *never* look like the picture on the cake-mix packet, nor do they ever vaguely resemble the cook-book's photo of whatever cake you are making. I wonder how much the well-known photographer, David Bailey, charges to make those damn cakes look so *huge*, when in reality they come out of the oven about 2 cms thick?

Yes, that's right, 2 cms thick … and then the Twat was supposed to slice it in half and put the filling in. Now this was going to be interesting, especially as the Twat couldn't find the separate sachet containing the ingredients for the filling. I expect that it had ended up being incorporated into the rest of the cake.

Nice. I was thoroughly assured that the cake mix had been properly whisked, although I couldn't help but ask myself: *Why on earth did I ask him to make me a cake in the first place?*

I should have known better than to let the Twat continue with his baking when he asked me for a cake tin. I got one out of the cupboard for him, and to make life even easier, I chose one of those cake tins whereby you can detach the base once the cake is cooked.

I showed the Twat how this worked and his reply was: "Oh, so that's what that's for. I normally scratch the cakes out."

Did I back out? Did I? No. Flabbergasted, I decided that my best option was to go upstairs and hide. This wasn't enough, though, as the Twat kept coming upstairs and asking me what the difference between beating and blending was, how does one grease a cake tin, and last, but not least … where the oven was.

Once again, the Twat had made another offer to help, but this time in the kitchen, and Christ alive, my boyfriend really knows how to make a mess. If you live with a man who can whip up a mean meal and yet leave you cleaning the walls, the kitchen surfaces, the oven, the floor – not to mention doing the washing-up or the tedious and mind-numbingly dull job of filling up the dishwasher – then take back the lease of your kitchen and throw him out. Personally, I can think of nothing worse than tidying up somebody else's mess, so if you want a good meal, then eat out.

Your partner may have all the best intentions in the world when it comes to cooking for you, but if it means leaving you to clear up after him then it's not such a good idea after all, especially when those delicious curry sauces are coming ready-made out of a jar.

TWAT HEALTH

THE LUNGS

Men fall into two categories with regards to health: there are those who think that they are on the brink of death should they so much as sneeze, and those who are on the brink of death but think it's macho to go around saying that they are fine. Beware of those who think that they are macho, because, to be quite honest, they aren't.

My boyfriend falls into the latter category. I think he feels that, as he was once a member of the busiest mountain rescue team in England, he can therefore save his own life and doctor himself. This, obviously, is utter bollocks, and there is no one better to witness that than myself. There is, however, a positive outcome from the Twat's past with the rescue team and that is that he is pretty good at diagnosing other people's ailments and suggesting what should be taken, or if the intervention of a doctor is necessary.

Several years ago, as we were out wandering around in the centre of Brussels getting the Christmas shopping in (with the rest of Brussels, it appeared, judging by the miserable looking hordes of shoppers weighed down by carrier bags), I realised that the Twat's pace had slowed down incredibly. He couldn't even keep up with me as I charged ahead, trying to avoid the busy crowds. As I slowed down to walk with him, he suddenly collapsed against me. I had no option other than to try and throw him onto a nearby bench. His face was ashen grey, but as he pulled out a cigarette, coughing deeply as he lit up and all the time assuring me that he was fine, I let it go.

I joined the Twat and lit up, too. It was a cold day but as his cough worsened and he started coughing up bucket-loads of phlegm, his hollow cheeks looking greyer by the minute, I started wondering how I could blackmail the man into going to hospital as he was clearly having a bad asthma attack. That's correct. The man smoked at least twenty cigarettes a day despite being an asthmatic. The idiot. So I decided to go home, stopping on the way at the hospital so as to sort out the Twat's health insurance, which was easy to do as he didn't understand a word of French.

When he twigged, whilst standing in the middle of A&E, that I was, actually, admitting him into hospital, the Twat slowly started backing out of the building, assuring me that it was just a cold. I replied sternly, for all and sundry to hear that, if it was just a cold, then "should any one of my children catch it, we are well and truly fucking over. Finito. You, Quarsan, go back to England and that will be that." He blanched even more and gave in, and he ended up having thorough tests involving scales, a stethoscope, needles and a plastic toilet roll. (Don't ask.)

I learned that a man of the Twat's height and size should carry up to six litres of air in his lungs. His barely contained two litres, hence his grey pallor. The oxygen level in his blood was so low that the doctors decided to keep the Twat in on the basis that the man should, actually, be dead, and this time he couldn't argue as he couldn't communicate unless in Swahili, but unfortunately for the Twat, nobody understood Swahili.

The Social Services came in to try and sort out the best way to get Quarsan on to some kind of health insurance so, leaving him in the hands of some very capable doctors, plus two extremely helpful women who were sorting out his insurance, I left to go home and feed the kids, promising to come back later with some overnight clothes and toiletries, as that was all he needed.

The Twat spent an enjoyable week in hospital, where he managed to bribe the woman who delivered the meals to bring him two pots of coffee rather than just the one. Even better, he shared a room with another man whose wife would come in with stacks of porn magazines on a regular basis for her husband. He did not, however, appreciate a certain visit that I made on the Friday night, when I turned up with a friend from France after having knocked back a couple of bottles of wine. As we bounced from wall to wall breathing fumes of alcohol all over him, he ended up leaving the room to watch TV. When the Twat came back, he found my friend lying on his bed with the oxygen tubes up her nose.

He was not amused.

When the Twat was discharged from the hospital, armed with

Ventolin and some other drug which contains steroids, thus causing heavy weight gain over the years, I only allowed him back in the house on the promise that he'd never smoke again. He agreed to this, somewhat half-heartedly. Of course, being the sort of man that he is, that is, not the sharpest knife in the drawer when it comes to going behind my back, he'd often nip out for a cigarette in the garden, thinking I was occupied elsewhere in the house. There I would be, tidying up the bedroom, and my dear partner would be puffing away right underneath the bedroom window, sending wafts of smoke into the room. I'd end up opening the window and shouting at him until he left for shelter at the bottom of the garden. Yet he still carried on having a 'secret' puff just outside the bedroom window, until I resorted to desperate measures to try and deter him. I bought a packet of water bombs which I would liberally throw at him, at the expense of his book and cigarette. He soon began to learn.

THE TOOTH

A year or so later, having almost given up the cigarettes, I noticed that Quarsan was knocking back Amaretto at an alarming level, so it came as no surprise to me when he asked me for an aspirin.

"Bad hangover?" I enquired.

"No, toothache," was the pitiful reply.

Apparently, my poor, dear boyfriend had been taking two aspirins at a time, along with a large glass of Amaretto, to ease the pain. When I mentioned seeing the dentist, however, the Twat merely grunted and told me that he'd have none of that now that the pain had eased off, and besides, dentists were for 'wusses'.

The following morning I woke up only to find that the man had vivid red marks across his forehead from where he had been clutching his head during the night, trying to ease the pain by putting pressure on it. I thought it pointless bringing up the issue of seeing a dentist again and so made an appointment for the man myself, called him from work and told him that my dentist was expecting him at midday. This time, the twat didn't even argue, and even went again the following week for 'the wiring'. Apparently, it was something to do with a nerve... Ouch! No wonder he was in so much pain.

THE RASH

The tooth incident was followed by the case of the 'itches'. One morning, the Twat woke up with a bright red, puffed-up face that itched from here to Antwerp. He looked very similar to a Teletubby, in fact. He was in severe discomfort, but the mere mention of seeing a doctor was shunned. It almost felt like having a door slammed in my face, though I was only trying to help. The second night I was kept awake by the Twat scratching away at any part of his body that itched, which, unfortunately, happened to be most of it. Each time I fell asleep again, I'd be woken up by the Twat having a shower as a way to relieve himself of the discomfort.

Nothing worked. The Twat refused to have a bath in bicarbonate of soda. Yes, it sounds weird, but that's what they plonk babies with chicken pox in over here. I've yet to see calamine lotion on any shelf in this country. This state of affairs continued until the day somebody left a comment on my site suggesting that the Twat take some strong anti-histamines. Although my helpful correspondent wasn't a doctor, he just happened to have a box of these very same anti-histamines in his possession. As they were very strong ones that can't normally be bought over the pharmacy counter, the Twat accepted.

The man offering help lived nearby and so Quarsan arranged to drop by and pick them up. He paid for them and took them religiously according to the instructions on the accompanying piece of paper, yet nothing happened. He still looked like a tomato and couldn't stop scratching himself.

Things got worse. I arrived home from work one day to find that he appeared to be hallucinating, asking if one of my daughters was in the house when she was clearly at school. He started rubbing his palms together as even they were affected by the rash, and the noise was diabolical at night. Typically, though, the Twat reckoned I was the person at fault.

"You've changed the soap powder 'aven't yer?"

"No, I'm still using the same soap powder as before."

"Fookin' 'ave."

"NO, I FUCKING HAVEN'T."

The itching slowly subsided and went away, but the cause of it is still a mystery to us all, especially as he developed some sort of a rash when he first moved here – nothing quite so bad, but nevertheless, you could see it was a rash. I reckoned that it could well be down to the éclairs that he was eating. He was scoffing several a day and so, much to his disappointment, I banned him from buying any more. The filling in éclairs in this country is pretty rich in eggs, to which he is allergic. After three weeks, once the rash had cleared, I let the Twat eat éclairs again. He was fine. My bet is that food is allergic to *him*.

THE COLD

When Quarsan gets a dose of the common cold, he is a very bad patient and just wants to be left alone to sleep it off. He doesn't take kindly to offers of tea and honey, aspirin or other hot drinks and gets verbally aggressive until he achieves what he wants, which is peace and quiet. This, of course, suits me perfectly. Needless to say, when the Twat has a cold, it really doesn't help his snoring problem and the decibels are too great to be endured.

When you realise that your partner really is sick, don't 'mother him', simply cart him off to hospital, no matter how. Get a strong mate in to help you, call an ambulance – whatever it takes. Colds are part and parcel of life, unfortunately, and if your partner wishes to be left alone then it's time to get the glad-rags on and party till 2099 – or later. It depends in which direction your space-ship is heading.

AFRICA

THE FOOT

Quarsan doesn't only get sick in Europe – he also tends to fall ill in Africa, of all places. And to make things worse, each time that the Twat has fallen ill, he happened to be in his house in Tanzania. Under the Rift Valley and in the Bush. Well, where else?

The first time the Twat had to visit the local hospital was after a motorbike accident. Well, isn't that typical? Blokes and their motorbikes = disaster. It's a well-known fact. Except that the Twat's story is unique.

A woman *on foot* (important, please note) had been heavily engaged in conversation, as you do, with another woman.

Once the conversation had finished, she turned and walked into Quarsan on his bike, knocking him off. She wasn't injured but, in the process, he cut his foot quite badly. In severe pain, and flinching at the oozing flesh that was visible via the cut in his foot, the Twat pushed his bike to the side of the road and limped to the NGO (Non-Governmental Organisation) for which he was working at that time. The people there took one look at the Twat's foot and decided to drive him to the nearby hospital. The Twat insisted they stop *en route* at his home so that he could take some of his extra-strong painkillers and have a cigarette, naturally.

Well, we all have our priorities.

Once totally drugged-up and suitably smoked, the Twat was taken to the hospital where he was seen to by the chief doctor and nurse. By this time, the painkillers were beginning to kick in and the Twat couldn't feel a thing and was having quite a pleasant trip. The doctor and nurse had no idea about the Twat's indulgence in extra-strong painkillers and so, after the nurse had cleaned and stitched Quarsan up, who hadn't flinched once, she turned to him and told him, "You are a man."

Feeling mightily pleased with himself, the Twat hobbled out

of the hospital. As he waited for somebody to drop by and give him a lift home, he gave several coins to a nearby child to buy him a couple of bottles of beer to pass the time away.

As the hospital was close to the Twat's home, the doctors would often drop by in the afternoons to take his blood pressure and check on how he was doing. A week later, the chief doctor claimed the Twat to be a magician as not once had he managed to take his temperature, despite having intended to on every visit. Instead, each afternoon had turned into a social occasion. The doctors were given tea and chocolate cake, light banter, a blood-pressure reading, but hadn't managed to get near him with a thermometer – until the night when the chief doctor managed to take it at last and discovered that it was an astronomical 46°C. Being a bloke, the Twat refused to go to hospital as "it was full of sick people", and besides, he had his house-girl to look after him and, if necessary, the NGO for whom he worked would help him out. Typical.

This didn't go down well with the chief doctor and so the very next day, the Twat received a visit from Nurse Fran. Nurse Fran belonged to the Chagga Tribe, a Tribe that is seriously not to be messed with. She looked at the Twat and said, "Come with me."

And he had no choice, even though he tried.

"But they won't let me smoke in hospital," was his main objection.

Nurse Fran soon quashed that with, "I'll let you smoke."

And it was Nurse Fran who saved his life, as the Twat was in hospital for a week on antibiotics. They would keep his temperature down for a few days and then it would flare up again. Once back in his house, still on antibiotics, the same problem continued until, despite Quarsan's protests about not wanting to be treated by an English doctor, the NGO finally sent the Twat back to the UK to recuperate and get the expert physiotherapy that he so badly needed.

TYPHOID

But had the Twat learned from this experience that it's not a good idea to trifle with your life? Oh no, because the very next time that he was back in Tanzania in the little rural village where he lived, bad luck struck again. One night he found himself having difficulty sleeping and felt as if he was coming down with something like flu. He felt feverish and cold and woke up freezing, so he got up, made himself some coffee, wrapped himself in a blanket and sat outside his house reading a book as the village came to life. As the villagers set off to their small farm plots, the Twat sat there bidding them all a good morning until a friend from the nearby NGO stopped by on a motorbike and offered the Twat a lift to the hospital in case he had caught malaria.

Not even half a kilometre down the road, the motorbike ran out of petrol and so a passing villager offered to take the Twat to the hospital on the back of his bicycle. They were almost at the hospital but the Twat was beginning to lose all sense of balance and so tried staggering the rest of the way only to be saved by a passing car which literally dropped him in front of the hospital. From thereon, the Twat made an appointment with the doctor, who actually happened to be the dentist, went back outside for a cigarette and a beer until he was called in where he was immediately diagnosed with typhoid. The doctors almost had to plead with the Twat to be admitted, knowing his dislike towards hospitals, especially as this time Nurse Fran was not around to allow him to smoke. During his stay, the Twat only just managed to get around going out for a cigarette and a beer by walking past the nurse's room on all fours .... even if the nurses did yell at him as he did so since they could see a drip going past the window – but without a person pushing it.

The day following the Twat's admission to hospital, the doctor who diagnosed him came down with typhoid as well...

Quarsan's medication didn't seem to be doing much for him as, although he felt fine during the day, his fever would flare up again during the night, and it got to the point where he couldn't recognise people that he knew well. It got to a stage that neither the doctors nor nurses actually thought that he was going to make it as one particular nurse, aptly named Angel, would come in every evening with the entire nurse crew, each passing by the Twat's bedside and saying *"Pole Sana"* ("We're very sorry"). This would be followed in the morning by the hospital guards visiting him, all thoroughly pissed and clutching spears, and then the local priest would make his daily visit.

Death wasn't far away, it seemed.

But life got better as the Twat was joined by roughly half the village as there had been a malaria break-out which meant that the Twat was not only sharing the ward with tuberculosis sufferers, but those with malaria as well, now. Fortunately, the doctors were extremely good, finally let the Twat out after only five days and he waved his final farewell to that particular hospital as he left on the back of someone else's motorbike.

The next day, someone from the nearby NGO popped around to see how the Twat was doing, and also to drop off the bill which amounted to the costly sum of around £10. Not feeling totally 100%, Quarsan decided to go to the bank in Babati the following day so as to pay the bill which almost put him back into hospital again as the 'bus' (pick-up truck) that he took back into the village started heading rather fast into a ravine. Too fast, to be precise, as the brakes had failed. It ended up flipping over and landed in a deep ditch, but, as luck would have it, our faithful survivor managed to climb out with nothing more than a few bruises. There were no fatalities, just the odd broken bone and, even luckier, the vehicle behind it happened to be full of Maasai, who treated the wounded and drove those in need of a doctor to the hospital.

The Twat went home, bruised and shaken, but nevertheless ready to pay his hospital bill the next day.

> Either the Twat is lucky or unbreakable, but quite frankly, when he is ill or 'broken', I no longer worry. Take Nurse Fran as an icon to live up to, and you won't be taken for a caring, dithering idiot. You will be seen as somebody who does her job.

MENTAL HEALTH

CLIMBING ACCIDENTS

Personally, I would have thought that, as an ex-climber, the Twat would have had plenty of accidents. There was the time when he fell 150 metres and wedged his pick-axe in his thigh, his tracksuit bottoms of the time still bear the scar, as in an almighty hole. But that was the only accident he ever had climbing – everybody else was having them for him.

Apart from The Biggest Accident Ever.

And these are these are the exact words of the Twat...

"I climbed the entirely wrong mountain. We noticed when we got to the top and looked across and I said to my mate who was known as Due North Dave, 'You see that mountain over there? It's higher than this one.'

Due North Dave shuffled a bit and mumbled 'Yeah… it is … a bit.'

'Dave, we've climbed the wrong bloody mountain.'

'Well, Quarsan, we had better go back down and climb the right one then.'

And so they did.

Let me explain. Quarsan and Due North Dave, so-called because whenever navigating he would tend to drift in the direction of magnetic North, regardless of the direction he was meant to be going in, decided to climb the Ruwenzori Mountains in Uganda. The fact that there was 'a bit of a war' going on at the time didn't deter either of them.

Whenever the Twat went on climbing expeditions abroad, he would always make the arrangements and book the flights, etc., but, as luck would have it, this time Due North Dave had gone ahead and made the flight bookings. Two dirt cheap tickets to Nairobi. Via Saudi Arabia. The tickets being so cheap made everything alright, despite having to change flights in Jeddah and having a baggage allowance of only 20 kilos which, if you are an experienced climber, you'll know is hardly enough.

On the appointed day, the Twat and Due North Dave arrived at Heathrow wearing their full mountaineering equipment, which included enormous boots and heavy mountaineering jackets with the pockets stuffed full of equipment such as carabiners, ice screws and other necessary equipment for ice-climbing. They handed over their pick-axes and crampons for safety during the flight, but their bags were full of rope and perhaps a change of clothes, too, so as not to go over the 20-kilo limit, and each of the two were wearing another 20 kilos of vital equipment.

It's all par for the course if you're a climber.

Once on the plane, they took off their heavy boots and jackets, only to have to put everything back on again in Jeddah where they once again had to go through Customs. The Twat plonked his ice-axes and crampons on the desk whilst checking in, much to the alarm of the officer working there, who took one look at them and asked what on earth they were for.

"Climbing," replied the Twat. "We're going ice climbing."

"Why do you want to do that? And what is this for?" Not an unreasonable question from somebody who has only ever seen ice in a glass of Coca-Cola and had never seen snow, let alone a mountain.

The two climbers, suffering slightly from the heat under their heavy clothes despite it being five in the morning, were finally allowed on board the plane and set off for Kenyatta, Nairobi from where they took a taxi to Kampala and found a place to stay before setting off to climb the highest peak in the Ruwenzori, Mount Stanley. These mountains are known for being shrouded in mist, which is why it wasn't until they were standing on the summit that the Twat noticed they were on the wrong mountain.

Now, why was the Twat so determined to go through all of this simply to climb a mountain? He had read that Mount

Stanley, the highest mountain in the Ruwenzori, is named after the famous explorer who first saw it. However, it turned out that Stanley named the mountain after his employer, the then editor of the *New York Times*.

The Twat couldn't resist climbing Mount Gordon Bennett.

Footnote: Due North Dave's girlfriend, Sue, was almost seven months pregnant when the boys left to run around mountains. When they returned to England five weeks later, Dave's girlfriend went to pick them up and Dave was completely unaware of a little practical joke that the Twat had suggested to Dave's girlfriend. As Sue approached the Twat and Due North Dave, Dave's jaw suddenly hit the floor. Sue had strapped a baby doll to her rather large belly...

The Twat at Play

TWAT'S ENTERTAINMENT

There is nothing a twat likes more than a good bit of monkeying around – which is normal, to be fair, as twats are ageless. Fortunately, as I have children, my partner is rather restricted as I like to tighten the reins somewhat. But when the children aren't here, I still feel as though I am looking after several five-year-olds encased in one body.

One year, we decided to give a friend of ours a surprise birthday party. We organised it with his girlfriend who was coming all the way from the South of France, bringing with her poppers (of the explosive kind), balloons and streamers, sparklers and a huge bag of fairly safe things that also went 'bang' and could be used indoors. How she got through Customs is anybody's guess, but then, she was flying with Ryanair. We liked her and wanted to meet up with her again, so we arranged with the Twat's mate, Ansh, to hold a barbecue at our place that was ostensibly in honour of *her*, so as not to ruin the surprise for the Birthday Boy.

As I didn't own a garden table at the time, we always lit the barbecue in the garden and took our food indoors to eat. This is common practice – unless, like us, you light it in the garage with the doors wide open while it pisses down with rain, as it usually does at our barbecues.

On this occasion, we were lucky with the weather. The kids really enjoyed the meal and had a great time. They were very talkative and friendly with everyone, which was probably due to the fact that there was a huge stash of explodable goodies in the middle of the table, and they couldn't wait to get their hands on them. This probably applied to my boyfriend and Ansh, as well.

We started off by throwing the streamers across the table. At this point, the birthday boy tried to set my house on fire by throwing a streamer directly across the path of a candle. After a mild panic over nothing, we carried on as if it had never happened, although I put my foot down when everybody wanted to light their sparklers in the house. As it was a warm night, I thought it best if we lit them outside, which was where the monkey business was about to begin.

As four adults and three children ran around the garden, waving sparklers about and chanting that we were fairies, I suddenly saw the Twat disappear into the house ... then re-emerge, clutching a box of leftover fireworks from the New Year and wearing a big grin.

This was the moment when I realised that certain people have no understanding of the firework code.

"It's fer wimps," was the Twat's response. This was worrying.

Very.

Ansh and the Twat grabbed anything that they could find in the box and started lighting them, without knowing what any of the items were as it was rather dark by then. One rather spectacular firework, obviously designed to be placed on something that couldn't be found, was balanced on the patio – until it fell under the chair on which the box of fireworks had been placed and carried on spinning around and around, sending out an incredible amount of sparks. Ansh ran to the end of the garden and disappeared, his girlfriend and I hopped onto the ledge of the French window and the kids all jumped onto a garden chair each.

"*MOVE THAT BOX OF BLOODY FIREWORKS, YOU TWIT!*" I bellowed. (There were kids around, you see.)

"Nah, it'll be OK."

"Just *MOVE* it!"

The firework was still going round and round in circles and sending out vicious sparks – so the Twat moved the box, leaving the rest of us choking in a yellow cloud of smoke that reeked of sulphur. By now, Ansh had reappeared from the dark end of the garden and was already starting to light another firework. Then he and the Twat started lighting rockets, dropping them into empty wine bottles and aiming them into people's gardens. After the last one had shot out into oblivion, we were quite happy to get out of the smoke and into the house for some birthday cake, with only one minor casualty. A burnt hole in the birthday boy's T-shirt.

The following day I found the plastic stand for the ballistic firework on the garden chair, next to an empty box of fireworks.

It is not, in my opinion, a good idea to let a twat loose with a box of fireworks. They neither realise the possible consequences, nor do they realise that accidents CAN occur. My feeling is that a twat with a cigarette lighter alone is a danger to society but, given a firework, I can only *imagine* the Great Fire of London erupting again. If you like dabbling with fire then, of course, do what you wish, but should you have any concern for the safety of others and yourself, then please, *please*, observe the Firework Code, because you know that your twat of a *partner* won't.

FASHION AND GROOMING

Clothes are a very good way of judging someone's character. You can tell if the person is rich, poor, fashion-conscious or just downright lazy. Should your date turn up wearing a pair of nylon tracksuit bottoms more suitable for going jogging round the block in than going out to dine at that new, bijou restaurant around the corner, it is easy to conclude what may have been going through his head, if anything at all.

- *They're the only 'trousers' I have.*

- *Everything else is dirty.*

- *What's wrong with them?*

- *I wasn't thinking.*

Dressing for the occasion does not mean getting out your designer-label clothes, but it does involve a little insight as to what would be appropriate, especially on that first date. A pair of twenty-year-old, second-hand tracksuit bottoms is unlikely to make a good impression, especially when accompanied by a pair of third-hand hiking boots that have seen the Damavand in Iran, the fells in Cumbria, the Simyen mountains in Ethiopia, the Ruwenzori in Uganda – to name but a few climbing haunts. Top that with a six-year-old T-shirt that was given away by a restaurant that had ordered too many in the hope of promoting the establishment, the logo of which is barely visible owing to numerous washes and its general battered state, and you could find yourself looking at an utter twat.

Why?

Those were, literally, the only clothes my boyfriend owned, bar a green fleece that had seen better days several decades ago, and his working clothes. When the Twat moved in with me in 2001, he had just enough clothes to fill two small shelves and considering he had been working on the fells in Cumbria when in England, you would have thought that he would have owned several jumpers and some heavy, water-proof trousers. But what did the Twat have instead? Two pairs of nylon tracksuit bottoms, six T-shirts, a fleece and some rather dubious underwear. One could argue that he obviously spends his money wisely, such as on holidays to go climbing, but when your bloke turns up wearing those clothes on your very first date, you can but grin and bear it whilst working out whether or not he's worth seeing again – especially as he has covered up this pitiful ensemble with his working jacket; a heavy labourer's coat with half of Cumbria on it.

A twat will not, in general, give a damn about his appearance, and further on into the relationship, other signs as to how fashion-conscious your boyfriend is, will gradually surface.

The Twat at Play

These are:

- *Socks with barely any soles.*

- *Underwear with no elastic left.*

- *T-shirts worn for weeks at a time.*

- *Tops with tomato sauce splattered all over them – and still worn.*

And so on.

Yet the poor soul has done no wrong, so you just have to live with it. The new fleece that you buy him will stay in the cupboard for weeks – possibly months – before he will deign to put it on, and when he does, it won't come off, not even for washing; such are the ways of a twat. I have never managed to understand my boyfriend's refusal to buy a new T-shirt, even though he did have five or six identical ones that he received for free. The logos on the T-shirts were all fading, most had cigarette burns in them and they had all lost the 'T' shape, which had me begging readers on my site that should they receive a free T-shirt that they really didn't want, I knew of a very needy home for them.

People were very kind, and the Twat was the recipient of quite a few T-shirts, some of which I suspect had actually been bought, but my ongoing battle between the Twat and his T-shirts is far from over.

Invariably, a twat's favourite fashion outlet is the local thrift shop, or a car boot sale where all the clothes have fallen off the back of a lorry, hence costing very little at all and giving the man the chance to buy about ten identical pairs of socks going for a quid each. The cheaper the better, and bugger the quality, is your average twat's point of view.

Buying clothes for a twat is extremely difficult and could almost be compared to buying a book for a blind man. The reason for this is because they simply aren't bothered and can quite happily carry on through life with their existing clothes, or at least, until those clothes fall apart – although a true, thoroughbred twat will not be put off there.

My boyfriend's current tracksuit bottoms have a split seam on the right thigh, a hole where he dropped his ice-pick into his leg during a mountaineering accident, cigarette burns plus burns from burning rhododendrons, and the material covering his arse has worn so thin that it is almost transparent. But that doesn't put him off – he even wears them to work.

When it comes to shoes, a twat will invariably stick to one type. In the Twat's case that happens to be hiking boots. Fair enough, they are old, the seams are breaking, but hell, if it keeps the mud off his feet he's a happy lad.

Just before the summer of 2003, the Twat happened to be working in the UK, so he visited his mate in Liverpool. This meant the inevitable trip around car boot sales on the Sunday, where the Twat bought himself an absolutely hideous pair of green, Dunlop plimsolls. These were bought because, he said, "It's easier to drive wearing these than my hiking boots." These plimsolls plagued my life for the sorry three years that they existed. Combined with the Twat's tracksuit bottoms and green fleece, I would beg for him to wear his hiking boots as he looked far too 'dainty', rather like an extremely tall leprechaun. But would he listen? Of course not.

Buying clothes for the Twat, however, is quite an easy and interesting exercise, thus putting him in a 'league of Twats' of his own. Early on in our relationship, I realised that as he didn't own a suit, there was no way that he'd be allowed into one of Belgium's registered buildings where we were to hold a conference the next day. On our way back home that very day, we stopped off at a shopping centre and I made the experience as painless for him as possible by picking on a cheap department store which sold everything. As we, or rather, I, looked through all the suits, I finally picked a couple that weren't too expensive and showed them to the Twat, who opted for the dark grey one rather than the navy blue. Fair enough – I'm not the person who is going to have to wear it. Or pay for it.

As he tried it on, I went to look for a belt and the incredibly patient saleswoman went in search of a shirt and matching tie *"pour monsieur"*. Her choice in shirts was fine, but the ties were terrible and I ended up choosing one that matched the shirt. The Twat let us choose for him as it was too difficult for him to do and, basically, he hadn't a clue. Finally, we had the goods, all chosen and paid for in under an hour which personally, I thought was pretty good going ... until I realised that the Twat also needed shoes.

I dragged him off to a nearby shoe shop that sells good quality footwear. The Twat was grunting something about why couldn't he wear his hiking boots until, much to our luck, we saw some shoes with a 50% discount on them. Oh joy! Not being a terribly picky person when it comes to choosing either clothes or shoes, he simply picked out a pair that I gave an 'OK' to, tried them on and was happy. He even bought himself a pair of Dockers for work in the UK (not that he'd been getting much work over there lately), and so what could have been a very painful experience turned into a rather pleasant one.

It is not, however, always the case.

When it comes to grooming, my boyfriend has the most dreadful sense of style, in that he refuses point-blank to pay more than a couple of quid to get his hair cut, a habit that he no doubt picked up from his days in Ambleside. Apparently, the local barber was a bit of a character and wouldn't let women into his barber's shop, telling them to go and get the shopping whilst swiftly pushing them out of the shop with his broom. He'd then turn to his customer and, in the Twat's case, it would be a matter of: "Now then lad, a number two, eh?" Pictures of the Twat just after leaving the place make him look like a terrorist and so if ever we are going to go somewhere or are expecting friends, then I make sure that he has had his hair cut a couple of weeks beforehand.

When Quarsan joined our household, he realised that I owned an electric razor that I used for my son's hair, so he gave up paying to have his hair cut altogether. Instead, he would either get my son to help him, or do the deed himself. When it comes to the latter activity, I am never too happy about it as something always goes wrong. Like the time the Twat forgot to put the comb on the razor and ended up looking like a prison inmate. On another occasion, when he was being aided by my son, Jake decided that his arms were starting to ache and so he left the Twat to finish off his half-shaven head himself. Each time the Twat shaves his own head I have to intervene, as there are always some clumps of hair that are longer than others, giving the impression of straggly bushes on a mountainside. A barber he is not.

An additional fixture to the Twat's face is the Worst Goatee In The World. The Twat simply doesn't look after it properly, has no idea as to how to trim it and yet will not part with it. Apparently, he used to have a full beard, something that I am

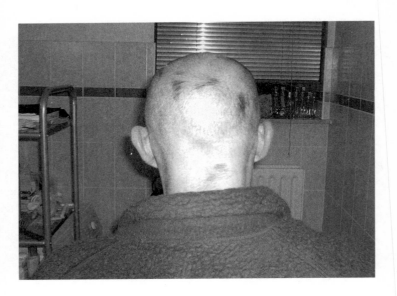

glad no longer exists, but he really should learn how to look after the extended growth of wiry hair that covers his chin and upper lip. Personally, I think that he owns this extension to his face simply to cover the fact that he lives up to England's reputation of having the worst teeth in the world, which makes the word 'goatee' all the more apt. If he shaved it off, I think I would be forced to make him wear a fake goatee, made out of real, soft hair. But as it is, it is nothing more than a wire brush stuck to the end of his face.

Fashion and grooming is a difficult area to cover, as the clothes that your partner wears are as much his choice as the clothes that you decide to wear and you know yourself that there is nothing worse than being told to *'put this on'* or *'put that on'*. A twat would not be a twat if he were well-dressed or well-groomed, depending, obviously, on the occasion, and you should enter this rather grey and potentially explosive area with great caution.

I started off by buying my boyfriend clothes for his birthday and for Christmas, but now that I think of it, there is a certain black jumper that I haven't seen for two years now, which was when I gave it to him as part of his Christmas present. It's not as if I can give him a voucher to a certain clothes shop as the man simply has no taste and I couldn't trust him to buy anything even halfway decent. So you have to tread delicately in this situation. Look at those items of your partner's clothes that really do need replacing and start from there, be it underwear, socks, T-shirts or even trousers. From there on, you can slowly transform your partner's wardrobe into something reasonably respectable, even if he does tend to wear the same clothes for weeks and weeks.

As for grooming, there isn't a lot you can do. If your partner tends to have very short hair, then buy an electric razor that is geared for cutting hair and cut it for him yourself. He will be pleased that he doesn't have to part with any money and, if you're lucky, will repay you in the bedroom. Or on the dining-room table. Or even in the kitchen. It's worth thinking about. Facial hair, should your partner have any, is another issue entirely. Personally, I have no problem with a man who goes two or three days without shaving. But a moustache must go, on the grounds that the hairs go up your nostrils when kissing. A goatee, depending on age, should also go for the same reasons, with the added factor that you don't like chomping on hair after a good snog. A man with a goatee that has existed for over twenty years should be encouraged to soften it with hair conditioner, so that you won't end up with a drastic rash all over your chin after a bit of horizontal jogging. And as for beards – get rid of it when he's asleep. The hairs between your teeth, the rash on your chin and the hairs up your nostrils after kissing – well, are they worth it?

GETTING THE TWAT FIT

Ever since Quarsan started taking his medication after a week in a Belgian hospital following a severe asthmatic attack, he has piled on the kilos. Not working on the mountains has obviously played a large part in this weight gain as the man was incredibly fit and a wall of muscle when I first met him due to his conservation work on the fells that involved lifting heavy rocks, carrying heavy bags of grass seed up the fells, not to mention the actual manual labour.

The campaign to get him fit again started with the great idea of going swimming together. But once the Twat found out that you have to wear proper swimming trunks and not shorts in public swimming pools – a law that was brought in several years ago as men swimming in bermudas find it easy to 'flash' their goods at young children – that plan went out of the window. There was simply no way that I could persuade the Twat to buy a pair of swimming trunks.

Next, I suggested jogging. Unfortunately, I couldn't accompany the Twat due to various bits of my body clanging around inside, and so one day I witnessed the Twat setting off on his first jog. He was back in ten minutes, red-faced and wheezing badly. I think that he managed to make it to the end of the road and back; it was his first and last ever jog.

Then I decided that it would be a good idea if we both started cycling. The Twat had been left a bicycle by a friend and I had one of my own – all that was needed to be done was to pump up the tyres.

Several weeks went by before I managed to convince the Twat to go out for a bike ride with me. Begrudgingly, the man finally got out his bike and off we went, heading for the fields. This new-found form of freedom went straight to his head and he spent a lot of the time trying to overtake me, flying past and making funny noises. It was like taking a rather young child out on his very first bike ride without stabilisers.

As we passed the first field with horses in, the Twat yelled out, "Ow do, 'oss?" which made me laugh so much that I fell off my bicycle, much to the delight of my boyfriend. This was only the first of my many tumbles that were to come that summer, each of which caused much merriment to the Twat and not the tiniest bit of sympathy.

There was the day when Hazel, Jake, myself and the Twat decided to cycle over the fields two days after it had rained fairly heavily. Despite the rain, the fields were already dry and hard as rock again. We found ourselves following a route that we used a lot and were familiar with, that incorporated a ditch in the middle of two fields that we were well used to avoiding. The Twat went past it first, then my son, my daughter and finally myself. On that particular day, I had chosen to ride Amber's bike and it wasn't until I was cycling past the tight border on the side of the ditch, now full of muddy water, that I realised that I wasn't going to make it and so had to brake. My daughter's brakes were new, meaning that rather than slowing down gently, as I was used to, the bike stopped dead and the only thing that I could do to avoid falling off was to put one of my feet down.

Of course, being me, I put the wrong foot down, meaning the one on the side where the ditch was. I felt myself slowly falling lower and lower into the pool of mud until I was lying in it, my other leg still over the saddle. I saw the Twat look back at me and then cycle on further until he was out of earshot, whereupon he and my son started laughing like maniacs. Hazel, on the other hand, looked back, jumped off her bicycle and pulled me out by the hand that wasn't covered in mud. My entire right leg was black, my left leg looked pretty bad too and the most sympathy that I got out of the Twat was, "What's it like cycling with mud up yer crack?" I never forgave him for his lack of compassion in that certain situation. The twat.

On several of our other cycling expeditions, the Twat would tell me, "I can feel the thunder" or "I can feel the rain – it's going to rain in half an hour". I'd often ask him how he could tell. I know that I can more or less predict rain, but the Twat would be dead set on the weather changing for the worse almost to the exact timing – because he comes from Cumbria. And because it rains so much in Cumbria. And because my boyfriend used to work on the fells where he could see the rain clouds approaching, which meant that he could forecast the weather. Not to mention having worked on the Mountain Rescue Team, where the weather was often a problem when trying to rescue a climber, which obviously gave the man some sort of superior powers over anyone else when it came to weather issues.

I'd ask where the swallows were, as that's always a sure sign of rain as they come down to get the bugs that are usually the first indication of a storm approaching, but the Twat would put me in my place with, "We don't need swallows in Cumbria to tell whether or not it's going to rain, lass."

Despite the fact that we were in Flanders, not Cumbria, it didn't seem to deter him. He would merely put on a strong Cumbrian accent and tell me the weather forecast. But somehow I never quite believed him, as it never did end up raining – it was just an excuse to take a short cut and get home the quick way. The lazy sod.

There was very little hope for him until the day that he went out and bought some weights with the hope of building up his biceps again. The most that he has done is remove them from the box and leave them in the living room by the French windows, which is probably the most exercise that he has gained from them. Even my son has used them more than he has, which can only leave me to conclude that the man really is lazy.

And so, being the Queen Bitch that I am, I put the Twat on a diet just after Christmas. Over the Christmas period I noticed that I had lost weight and put it down to drinking less. Oh yes,

I tend to drink less at Christmas, being a creature of abnormal habits. The Twat, on the other hand, was getting fatter than a Teletubby, his breathing was getting worse and so I told him that if he drank wine at lunch-time, then he wasn't to have any in the evening, and vice versa. I also applied this rule to myself, not that that lasted long.

Day One started out just fine – he even walked a couple of kilometres or so to a metro, instead of getting the nearest one to the office. As the Twat had a main meal at lunch-time, but with water rather than wine, he was allowed a tomato salad for supper with half a bottle of wine. So we started following his weight:

Day one: *Holy Crap!*
Day two: *Let's start swimming – I'll go with you.*
Day three: *I think my scales need more batteries.*

As the Twat does the cooking in this house due to my stepping down from that duty, I have found myself in a rather difficult position. In fact, I may well have to start cooking again as the Twat is a great believer in all things that don't involve anything more than heating up. Ready-made chicken korma sauce, pesto sauce, sun-dried tomato sauce, any Thai sauce available and so on, are an easy short-cut to cooking, and damn good they are too. But fresh is best, healthier and less fattening, so I may well have to get behind the wok, grill and oven and start cooking again simply to help let the Twat shed a few kilos. I'll leave it up to the sportier of my two daughters to provoke the man into actually moving his arse off the sofa. I've already denied him steak with Stilton sauce – it's the sauces that are served with food that pile on the kilos.

Trying to shed the excess kilos off your loved one is almost impossible unless you take over the kitchen, the cooking, start some ridiculous diet with him and spend an outrageous amount on a life-long membership at your nearest gym for the pair of you.

And that doesn't mean that he'll go along with it.

Dieting doesn't necessarily mean that you eat less – just more sensibly. Eat fresher foods, more vegetables and fruit, cut down on the pastries and wine and become an utter bore. If everybody did this, then there wouldn't be a market for microwaves, ready-made meals and take-away food. Fast-food 'restaurants' would quickly die a costly death and any restaurants still existing would serve minimalistic portions for the same price as they do now. But don't be fooled by this concept that was thought up by your partner while he was having a crap. You will not be ruining your country's economy – quite the opposite.

So how can you help your partner get rid of those extra tyres? There are certain foods and liquids that can be cut down on, obviously, such as anything that is deep-fat fried, crisps (potato chips for our friends across the pond), chips (French fries, also for our non-English native speakers), chocolate, beer, wine... The list really is endless, but quite simple to work out. Prepare break-fast for your loved one, and by this I do not mean a slice of toast and a cup of sugarless, black tea as this really will end up with him packing his pants, socks and various bits of clothing that he may own, and leaving without so much as a 'Sayonara, bitch'.

The easiest way to help your partner lose those kilos is by joining in with him. Just because his supper involves a plate of raw vegetables and a glass of water does not mean that you cannot sit opposite him and devour steak and chips, washed down with a bottle of the finest red wine. Exercise together, and by this, I mean driving alongside your partner as he jogs along, sweating for Europe, with the gentle encouraging words of "I thought I'd drive with you, darling, in case you collapse," as this will show just how thoughtful, loving and caring you are.

So far, I have managed to get my boyfriend to lose two kilos simply by insisting he does the shopping on foot and also acts as my personal waiter whenever my wine glass is empty.

THE TWAT AT CHRISTMAS

I hate Christmas, I really, really do. Twats seem to either love or hate it and if yours fits into the latter category, think yourself lucky. My boyfriend is one of those who can't get enough of Christmas. This is fair enough but, in a household that already contains three children, do I really need another one to cope with? To beg me to go out and buy a Christmas tree and suffer the consequence of pine needles under the carpet, in my shoes, down the side of the sofa and stuck in clothing for the following twelve months? No.

I remember all too clearly the first Christmas we ever spent together. I was gabbling fifteen to the dozen about how lovely the Grand Place (Central Square in Brussels, surrounded by beautiful, ancient buildings that were barely touched during the war) had looked the previous year. It had had an ice-rink in the middle and the most beautiful decorations all in gold, with the annual Nativity Scene at one end. I insisted on taking him to see this beauteous sight, so we trekked to the centre of Brussels only to find that there was no ice rink that year (if I remember correctly, it was due to the cost of the marriage of Prince Philippe to Mathilda), no golden statues, but instead, a huge Christmas tree surrounded by … life-size plastic cows and donkeys in four fake paddocks around the tree, with green, felt avenues in between the 'paddocks'. I was gutted. The Twat was mesmerised, especially when he saw that the Christmas tree had been decorated with life-size, inflatable sheep.

Shocked, and dying to move on, I tried to persuade the Twat to come and see the Nativity Scene, but he wasn't having any of that – he was utterly transfixed. It was so mad that it was brilliant in his mind, especially when he saw that the cows had lights inside them. We were definitely going back the next day during daylight so that he could take pictures, he said. At last I managed to drag him over to the Nativity Scene. The Twat didn't understand why there wasn't a baby, to which I had to explain that in Belgium, the baby is only put out on December 24 as that was when he was supposedly born. (Though that has changed since then and now the 'baby' is there from the start.)

He also thought that the mannequin dressed up as Mary was the most frightening 'Mary' that he'd ever seen, and admittedly, he had a good point. Unfortunately, they use the same one every year. It was then that my 'Newbie to Belgium' noticed, with a shock, that the sheep were moving.

"Well, of course – they're real. So is that donkey," I pointed out.

"Wowwwww ...."

Belgium, despite being shut on Sundays, was really starting to appeal to this man's Cumbrian heart and soul. I mean, real sheep!

I showed the Twat around what was then a relatively small Christmas Market. It has grown bigger and bigger over the years, making a season that I don't particularly like, into a time to look forward to. Especially welcome is the lady from Guadeloupe, who makes the best hot rum in the world, literally warming you from your head down to your toes. Quarsan enjoys visiting her stall each year, watching her as she sits there all day heating up her rum grog, adding to it and tasting it, getting more and more pissed as the day runs into the night, yet somehow making sure that she never gets short-changed, as she inspects the two euros that you hand over to her through her blood-shot eyes with her beautiful headdress fully intact.

Christmas Day can be such an ordeal, depending on the expectations of your family. If you have children, then they will want presents. If you have a television, then they will want what they see on TV. If you have a letter box, then they will want what they see in the mountains of pre-Christmas publicity. Failing all of that, they will want what their friends have. Normally, a twat would really like a gadget, but if your partner is anything like mine, he won't tell you which gadget, leaving you to try and pick his tiny little brain and guess what it is.

The solution? Don't get him anything – just make sure that you have dropped so many hints as to what you would like that your partner has little other choice than to buy at least one of the items on your list, knowing that if he doesn't, he may well end up being the turkey that year.

The only thing that I enjoy about Christmas is the Christmas Market. I am lucky that my boyfriend isn't that fussed about a big turkey spread on Christmas Day, but if you find yourself imprisoned in the kitchen on Christmas Day, sweating over an industrial-size turkey and all the trimmings, then it's time to sit down, turn up the music and pour yourself a large glass of wine. Let your partner look after the rest of the household.

TWAT SOCIAL SKILLS

Going to any social occasion with the Twat can be a very painful exercise indeed. When we are invited out in the evenings, whether it be for a drink in a pub, a meal some-where, a concert, or even a formal work event – which can be anything from attending a lavish reception with great food, to a quiet evening spent minding your p's and q's – the Twat will never want to go. Fair enough, we do live out of the city, which is where most of these events tend to happen, and it's a bit of a trek to get into the centre, but God almighty, there really is no need to sulk, be ratty, complain, moan and generally be a pain in the arse for twenty-four hours prior to the event. Especially when, once there, the Twat is suddenly utterly transformed from a sulky sod to a cheerful, high-spirited chap who gets along with everyone (most of the time, at least) and has a really good time.

He loves the receptions that I am often invited to, where the food is excellent, the plates are small and all the man requires is a bucket. He manages to smooth-talk so many people that, more often than not, we'll end up leaving a reception with a rather generous doggy-bag. This is such an excellent result that I can never resist having digs at him and trying to get him to apologise for having made me put up with his incessant complaining prior to the event. Having travelled so much to all sorts of weird and wonderful countries works in the Twat's favour, as it ensures that he can mix well with all sorts of people and discuss just about anything. And yet he will still complain till the cows come home before venturing out.

There is socialising with the man, and there is socialising... It's very difficult to go anywhere with someone whose best friend is a glove puppet called Quickos that my son received in his 'Happy Meal' at a burger joint and promptly gave to the Twat. My boyfriend and Quickos are inseparable, and the glove puppet could just as well be the son that my boyfriend will never have. Wherever the Twat goes, Quickos goes too. He has to be the best-travelled glove puppet in the world. He has been taken to India twice, Thailand, Scotland, Holland, Germany, the UK, France, the Maldives, Australia, China and even Qatar. Whoever takes him on holiday takes a series of photos featuring Quickos which get sent back to us – as does Quickos, folded up in two in a padded envelope. Each time the puppet leaves the house, the Twat will walk around feeling sad and listless and droning on and on about how much he misses Quickos. The puppet even has his own bed and sleeping bag and, naturally, his own blog.

Quarsan's second best friend is his computer, which must make him one of the world's most boring partners, although I know that I am not alone here. He spends hours sitting in front of the damn thing, and if he can't be found there, he can be found in front of the television and if not there, then there is a very good chance that he could be found heading in the direction of Holland.

I remember one day when I was ill in bed. I woke up and found myself absolutely parched. I called for the Twat to bring me up some water but it appeared that he wasn't in the house. Thinking that he had gone shopping, I called him on his mobile and asked where he was.

"I'm just entering Holland," was the reply.

All thoughts about how wonderful a man he is to have around when ill were soon thrown out of the window and he and Quickos found themselves sleeping on the sofa that night.

I did try another approach to socialising with Quarsan, and that was within our own family, with board games. Although I realised that playing Trivial Pursuit wasn't everybody's idea of a great evening in, I reckoned that it would get the children involved and help them get to know the Twat a little better. We tried it once or twice, with disastrous results and the odd hissy fit, then gave up.

As that had obviously been a dismal failure, I decided to buy a Scrabble board. Now, Scrabble is a game that I love, but I appear to be in the minority as the children's first language is French and Heaven alone knows what Quarsan's first language is. I managed to play several games of Scrabble with the Twat, resulting in arguments about how long I was taking to form a word and whether or not it was in the dictionary. That game, too, was rapidly given up as a lost cause, and the Twat would happily drift back to his computer, leaving me to try and play solitary Scrabble against myself.

Personally, I think that I have ruined any further chances of going anywhere with the Twat by giving in and letting him get those two satellite dishes installed on the roof of my house. This was probably the most stupid thing I could ever have done. Since they were installed, he has spent more time lying on the sofa clutching the remote control and zapping madly in between the 300 or so different channels, than anywhere else. He no longer goes to bed at the same time as me which means that, as long as I can sleep and am not woken up when he decides to come to bed, I am getting a good eight hours' kip each night, although he does get up early to watch the news. I am waiting for this phase to pass as the satellite dishes are a fairly new introduction into the Twat's life and, like all kids with new toys, he's bound to get bored – if I'm lucky.

Before moving to Belgium, Quarsan hardly drank at all and it was not unusual for me to find myself finishing a bottle of wine all by myself, then nursing a hangover the next day, depending on the quality of the wine. Little by little, the Twat started joining me in my evening beverage and I slowly managed to introduce him to Belgian beer, which is far superior to the cheap African stuff that he was used to. Because of the Twat's rather late introduction to alcohol, he is a pretty lightweight drinker and on the odd occasion he gets drunk, he does some incredibly funny things, such as the following typical display of Twatdom…

We had been invited to a friend's birthday party and everybody was drinking copious amounts of alcohol, the Twat included. If I'd thought the Twat would realise his alcohol limits at some point and stop drinking, I was wrong. Later in the evening, I found him clutching a bottle of Jack Daniels, waffling on about giant rats he'd seen out in the street and shouting, "Drink! Drink!" to anybody who passed by.

The party passed in a blur of alcohol. It was soon well after midnight. Most people had gone home, our host's girlfriend was already tucked up in bed and I was drunkenly looking for something to sleep on. There was no sign of my boyfriend, so I decided to curl up on the sofa – where, to my amazement, I was suddenly joined by our host. It appeared that when he had got up to go to the toilet, the wandering Twat had spotted a bed with an empty space in it and had crawled in. Next to our friend's girlfriend. It's a form of 'homing instinct' that suddenly kicks in when the Twat is really tired (or drunk), and that was exactly what he'd done. Homed into our host's bed and passed out.

Several hours later, our friend's girlfriend came and joined us on the sofa, exclaiming, "Christ your boyfriend snores heavily, Zoe – I've hardly slept a wink."

I'm not sure if we'll be invited to his birthday party again this year.

Ah, men and their jokes made at our expense; don't they love it? When I gave up cooking, the great joke was about whether or not I knew where the kitchen was and what, exactly, it was for, other than to pass through to get a bottle of wine from the garage. Hysterically funny, or so my boyfriend thinks. The trouble is that when you have been living with someone for a certain number of years, you start to find their humour funny, too, even the outrageously embarrassing atrocities that they are likely to come out with at cocktail parties in front of ambassadors and other such high-ranking persons. If your partner does this to you, be a sport and laugh with him – it will reflect better on you and make the two of you look like a fun couple.

Besides, you can always hit your partner afterwards. Should your partner have a rather close relationship with a soft toy, it really is no worse than the one he may have with his computer – providing, of course, that he doesn't start sending his computer all around the world. And should your boyfriend fake an allergy to nights out on the town, ignore his complaints and constant moaning because, if it gets too much, you do realise, don't you, that you can leave him at home with his satellite TV.

The Twat
at Work

TWAT JOBS

What my partner did for a living when he lived in the UK and Africa has always been something of a mystery to me, as 'conservation' is a rather wide title for almost anything to do with nature. There again, it could cover the conservation of old buildings or the restoration of collapsing houses that are 'listed'. When the Twat told me the name of his business, 'Sustainable Trails', I was even more confused. What, exactly, *did* he do?

Using traditional methods, he repaired footpaths on the fells in Cumbria, as well as in Tanzania, where he was employed by FARM-Africa to help teach the villagers in the Rift Valley to repair the footpaths, especially those that led to the local hospital, something that the Twat is very happy that he did. When the Twat was working in Cumbria, there were only about 20 people in total who had this skill, which had been rediscovered and pioneered by the National Trust. Dry stone walling was also involved, as was the building of drains. So the Twat wasn't a complete idiot after all, but his business fell apart after the outbreak of foot and mouth disease.

I used to refer to his job as 'the Twat standing on a mountain throwing rocks around – a bit like Obelix', but now that he has actually explained to me what he did, I must admit I am slightly in awe.

The Twat also worked as a volunteer on the busiest Mountain Rescue Team in England, which kept him fairly busy. As he spent most days up a mountain, the National Trust let him have a pager and a radio from the Rescue Team in case he was anywhere near a reported accident. Several of the incidents have been rather memorable. For instance, there was the time when a young South Asian girl had hurt her leg. The Team Leader, who came from Bury and sported a very thick, northern accent as well as an excellent bedside manner, tried to reassure the girl.

"Now then Petal, there's no need to worry, everything's going to be alright, Petal. Now just take some of this, Petal, that's right, we'll have you home in no time," he said soothingly as he offered her some anaesthetic gas.

The Team saw to the young girl's leg whilst the Team Leader carried on talking, in his heavy Cumbrian accent.

"That's excellent, Petal, won't be a minute now, you just lie down, Petal and we'll 'ave yer right as rain in no time. That's great, Petal, feeling any better?"

The girl just stared at the Team Leader in total and utter disbelief, so he asked her, "What's the matter, Petal? Does it hurt somewhere else too, now, Petal?"

"How did you know my name?" replied the bewildered girl.

If, as in my case, your partner has moved away from his original home to live with you, there is naturally the milestone of obtaining a job that has to be overcome. We hadn't expected this to be so difficult. The Twat was expecting more conservation work back in the UK, but many of the jobs only lasted two or three days – hardly worth flying back for. And so he became lazy and grew used to the life of mornings spent with his computer, until a chance arose for him to work in my office.

Since Quarsan started working there as the IT Manager, things have only got worse. Wanting to make a good impression, he sorts out everybody else's problems before getting around to mine, by which time I've left for home as I only work part-time, unfortunately. He's a bloody sod to work with and seeing as we live together as well, I can't help but get stroppy with him, something I wouldn't do if he were someone else.

The Twat gets grumpy and blames me for the malfunctioning of my email that he set up. He spent ages trying to sort out the office's new laptop. Things kept going wrong so he would sit there, swearing and being a general twat in every sense, until I'd had enough and ordered him to go off and work elsewhere – anywhere but my office. IT guys often tend to be pains in the butt anyway, but when your employer's IT manager is your own partner, that pain in the butt will be unbearable.

Ladies, no! Do. Not. Ever. Work. With. Your. Partner. Think of those quiet evenings at home when he has gone out with his mates to watch the football – don't you enjoy them? Work is the same thing, apart from the fact that you have to work, that is. It's your little niche. Do you really want your partner invading it?
No, I thought not.

DIY AND A TWAT

This chapter could basically be left totally empty as the two just do not get on together. Unless you call bleeding a radiator 'DIY' and, even then, it can be so difficult to get a twat to learn the basics of bleeding a radiator that you will find yourself more or less stuffed. It is best to either start learning the joys of the use of power drills or get the telephone number of a good handyman.

As the Twat wanted to look as if he knew what he was doing, he decided to drive all the way to Holland, a place he travels to rather too frequently for my liking, rather than to the nearby DIY store, and purchase a box of screwdrivers. Although the purchase was, and has been, fairly useful, in his view he needed those screwdrivers to bleed the radiators with, despite the fact that I manage to do it with a simple knife. Woman 1: Man 0.

The transformers for the lights on the landing and in the hallway were both broken. This meant that as soon as the sun went down, this well-used area was plunged into darkness, making going up and down the stairs a hazardous occupation. The Twat would continually point out this very obvious fact to me but wouldn't do anything about it, as buying new lights would mean a trip to IKEA, and we all know his thoughts about the Swedish store with the tongue-twisting product names.

I finally managed to get my own way by mentioning that if we went to IKEA, we could also buy a second CD rack as the first one was full, mainly of bootleg copies of CDs that the Twat had bought in Liverpool. (This was in the days before we needed a third one.) Cheered by this idea, the Twat led me around the huge store to get the lights and pick up the CD rack, without my being allowed so much as a peep at anything else. That's the Twat for you.

The installation of the lights didn't take place until several weeks later, and involved a lot of profanity and a fair bit of abuse aimed at me, as Quarsan was convinced that I hadn't turned off the electricity in that part of the house. Annoyed that he didn't trust me and my fuse box I simply stood there, passing the Twat the odd screwdriver that he needed at any given time, as well as taking the transformer from him and giving him the new one to fix up. The job was a fairly simple one, but I was a bit short to do it myself, so played the part of 'the person who receives the broken goods and passes on the new goods'.

Several swear words later, the Twat had finally installed the lights and was still alive to tell the story. Parts of the old fixture are still nailed to the walls to this day, though, as he couldn't be bothered to take them down. I suppose that will be left for the handyman to do. After that, the Twat tried to excel himself by putting together the CD rack. Now, I have always found that men are pretty useless at putting IKEA furniture together as they can't tell the difference between the lengths of the various screws, which are always thrown into the same bag as all the rest. Men simply can't work this out. Several hours passed until, finally, the Twat asked me to help him stand the CD rack up. He had actually managed to follow the instructions and put together the various bits of wood that were once a flat-pack and now just needed the shelves to be slotted in. A miracle.

The Twat has managed to surprise me on other occasions, too. He once fixed my son's glasses temporarily by using a stapler to fix the arm back on when there wasn't a screw small enough for the job.

Then there was the time when he unblocked the basin in the bathroom using a couple of very long skewers. To be honest, it was what Quarsan pulled out that alarmed me – other than the usual clumps of hair, he also managed to pull up an entire glass that was down the pipe. In pieces, naturally. I should note that the basin in question no longer has a metal cover with holes in it over the plug to stop large items, such as pieces of glass, falling down it. Where it went to is a mystery. This is a bit of a nuisance, especially as this basin happens to be in the kid's bathroom. I can only assume that the Twat knows more about it than he is prepared to say.

On the downside, when faced with a washer, or asked to clean the filters on the taps, the Twat is at a loss. He did, however, put a new layer of silicone around the bath and shower tub once, and once it will remain as the messy results have been an embarrassment to me ever since.

If you happen to live with someone who is as bad at DIY as my boyfriend is, then either do it yourself or pay for an odd job man to come round and do the job properly. Is your relationship worth throwing down the pan for the sake of an unchanged washer? A blocked toilet? Unvarnished window frames? Well, I didn't think

so, either, so you must learn how to do it yourself, or else pay someone to do it. I do, however, think that it is quite right of you to moan if your partner is incapable of changing a lightbulb, but that says a lot about you as well because changing bulbs is one of the easiest jobs in the world. Easier than cooking, even.

However, no woman should risk breaking her nails, or even getting her hands dirty, if there is someone else in the household to do it for them. This is not a fact that is easy to convey to a twat, but keep trying – unless, that is, you actually enjoy doing those grubby household jobs yourself.

THE TWAT AND TRADESMEN

It is a very English thing to give anybody who is coming around to do some work for you a cup of good English tea, and even some biscuits, too. This is not so much the case in Belgium, as most manual workers can't wait to finish the job, leave and stop off at their local. I admit that I have always offered coffee or whatever to my cleaning lady and to the handyman who comes around every now and then, but the

Twat's approach to labourers is quite unique.

From what I have seen, the Twat spends an awful lot of time getting to know the person that I am paying to do something in my house, chatting, getting cups of coffee and so on. I would have nothing against any of this if it wasn't for the fact that I was being charged for the time spent 'socialising'.

The first time my cleaning lady came round, the Twat was running everywhere, making her cups of coffee and trying to engage in conversation with her about where she comes from and isn't it a lovely country. This was really quite amusing to watch as it was more of a one-way conversation than anything, as my cleaning lady hardly speaks French, let alone English. But gesticulation can get you far, it seems, and little work was done that day.

Several years ago, my Polish handyman came around to sand and varnish my window frames. He is a hard and honest worker and I have used him a lot in the past – that is, until Quarsan came into my life. I am not saying for a minute that the Twat is now doing the jobs that my handyman did, although it would make my life a lot cheaper if he did, or even could.

So when my handyman arrived to help with the window frames, the Twat was in better luck, as my useful Pole speaks French and English fairly well. A lot of coffee was drunk that day, a lot of cigarettes were smoked, a few beers were knocked back in the afternoon and I parted with more euros than I should have done. He had to come back again the next day to finish the job, but fortunately, both the Twat and I were at work.

Unfortunately, a friend who happened to be visiting and house-sitting for us that morning has the gift of the gab and was just as bad as the Twat. He very quickly befriended my handyman and proceeded to give him all sorts of tips about England, as he was going there the following week to do some work for somebody else. As my friend sat outside typing on his laptop, he and my handyman engaged in heavy conversation, drank mugs of coffee and smoked a hell of a lot. Needless to say, the job was still not finished, but at least my handyman didn't start over-charging me; the two of them simply drank me out of coffee and used up all the oxygen in the garden.

Another labourer that the Twat decided to take a liking to was the man who accepted an awful lot of money to sort out my heating and hot water problems. Rik has visited my house several times now, mainly because he has forgotten to do something that he had promised to do, but he is such a cheerful person. I would be, too, at the rates he charges.

The first time that the Twat met him was when, although I could run a hot bath, I was having trouble getting hot water out of my shower. Cheerful Rik turned up with his son in tow and was promptly sat down by the Twat and treated to a cup of coffee and a chat all about where he comes from in Belgium. Once the Twat had finished his coffee, there was no need to keep Cheerful Rik from doing his work and so I led him towards my water heater and told him all about the problem; lukewarm water in the bath and freezing cold water in the shower, probably due to the pipes being blocked by limescale.

While Cheerful Rik checked out the water heater and discovered that the problem was all down to a broken valve, the Twat continued babbling away as to where he comes from and how wonderful the Lake District is. My personal take on this camaraderie is that it is probably the last time I ever employ a workman who speaks English, especially as he only charged for one hour and that came to a hefty €360. Cheerful

Rik did, however, show the Twat how to bleed the radiators, told him how often to do it, and then almost made a dash for the door before the Twat offered him a beer.

My boyfriend was clearly bonding with the people of Belgium, especially as Cheerful Rik was called back a year later due to more heating problems. He came around to fix the boiler which clearly had a problem as even the Twat and I were sharing a bath in the morning by heating up the kettle twice and adding a bit of cold water. The temperature in the house had dropped and as I prefer that the Twat remains as far away as possible from any vital item of household equipment (other than the cooker, that is), I checked the boiler myself, only to find that the pilot light was off and I couldn't turn it back on. Suggestions from the Twat such as, "Here, use my lighter", were met with an icy stare. I had no option other than to invite my boyfriend's friend, Cheerful Rik, back into our house.

He fixed the problem and left rather hastily – perhaps worried that he may get caught up in some casual banter, and this was where cheerful Rik made a terrible mistake. He forgot to switch the radiators back on so I had to call him back once more. This time, Cheerful Rik actually showed the Twat how to get radiators that like to remain stone cold warm again, but the Twat appears to have forgotten how to do so – probably in the vain hope that I will pay for his chum to pop around every time. Fortunately, I have a neighbour who is pretty good, if not brilliant, at these sorts of things – although he isn't always that available seeing as he is a pilot.

As with policemen, it is not wise to let your partner anywhere near anyone who visits your house and ends up charging you, as the hours 'worked' will be more and the work done will be less, with the inevitable result that you end up parting with more money than normal. However, should your partner get to the person that you are paying before you do, make sure that you pee in his beer and then get him to pay.

The Twat on Life, the Universe and Everything

TALKING TO THE POLICE

We haven't had many brushes with the Law, as it were, but each time that we happen to be filing a complaint, or even simply talking to the police, the Twat invariably puts his foot in it, joking away and not only wasting the policemen's time, however bored they may be, but my own as well.

The first time we were actually stopped by the police was when we had dropped someone off at the airport and were on our way home. There were several police cars on the road and each officer was pulling vehicles over, looking, I suspect, for illegal immigrants or stolen cars. The only illegal person between the two of us appeared to be the Twat – and the car wasn't ours, either. So I watched my boyfriend blag his way out of that one.

The Twat explained in great detail that the car wasn't ours officially, we'd just been lent it by a friend who is in Beijing for several years. This saved us the bother of explaining that the Twat simply hadn't been arsed to get round to actually buying it, as the exchange of papers would have been costly. The fact that none of the car papers were in the car, either, was overlooked and the policeman was very nice about it all, probably because he was pissed off that it wasn't a stolen car.

Then the Twat had to do a little explaining about his (English) driver's licence. It was issued in the early '90s and has no photograph on it. It was obviously the first time the policeman had seen such a licence and it baffled him somewhat, so the Twat promised that he'd get it renewed and have his mug-shot put on it.

The policeman wasn't even bothered when my boyfriend couldn't produce his ID card as it's too big to put in his wallet, and let us go without a hiding. He was probably totally baffled, having never encountered anyone like the Twat in his life. As my boyfriend got back into the car after his chat with the fuzz, I asked him if he really was going to get a new driver's licence.

"Are you kidding?" he replied. "This one is valid until 2032."

That was a fairly painless confrontation with the police, but the next three got me close to hitting the Twat. The first occurred when I had to call the police because we'd spotted someone we knew trying to break into our neighbour's house. Six officers turned up and stood there watching as the Twat sat on a very, very drunk former friend of ours while I was trying to hold his feet still. It took them about ten minutes to decide what to do and take over, which they finally did by carting off the man to the Police Station. As this incident involved our neighbours, too, the Twat didn't put his foot in it. This time.

The following day, while the Twat was out, I received a call from our former friend and then a string of abusive calls from his mate, which led me having to call the police again in order to lodge a complaint. By this time, Quarsan was home and, though he probably thought he was doing the right thing, I really didn't need him sitting by me and adding his comments as I was trying to relate the content of the phone calls. All he was doing was confusing the situation – and the police officer – even further.

Me: "...And then he started accusing me of stabbing his neighbour in the back."

Policewoman: "It would have been impossible for him to have seen whether or not Mr Wino had been stabbed, as I saw that his back had been covered over with gauze."

Twat: "In English, if someone says that they have been stabbed in the back, it means that they have been spoken about unkindly by someone that they trust."

Me: "What the hell...? You weren't even here when I was being accused, and besides, that's not what it means in French."

Twat: "You see, Officer, in England... "

Me: "Would you be quiet? This is my complaint. Stop confusing the whole issue."

Twat: "And it's quite possible that Mr Wino may have meant that... "

Me: "I wasn't even talking to Mr Wino, I was talking to a Belgian. What are you on about?"

Many a confused glance passed between the police officers, until I managed to make my statement, no thanks to the

Twat. It's bad enough having children running through the house while you're trying to do something official, but a partner who just confuses the entire situation is something to avoid at all costs.

The third visit to the police station occurred not even a month later, but for a totally unrelated reason. This time we were there because the car that we had been kindly lent by a friend who had gone on holiday for a few weeks had been broken into overnight and the radio had been nicked, which really does give another meaning to Sod's Law. It is fair to say that it was me who stuck my foot into it this time, although I do blame my fetish for men in uniform.

The conversation went along the following lines...

The Twat: "Why does it happen? What can people get out of selling stolen car radios?"

Police officer: "Well, you get €20 here and another there – it all mounts up."

Me: "Yes, and I suppose if they are drug users, then that

could get them quite a lot. Not that I know anything about the costs of drugs on the market any more."

Police officer, suspiciously: "Any more?"

Feeling like a Class A drug dealer, though I have never touched hard drugs in my entire life, I blushed and stuttered something along the lines of: "Well, you know, we all smoked something when we were 17... "

I had just decided to shut up and stop digging an even deeper hole for myself when the Twat put his hand gently on my thigh and said: "We'd better not mention the bank robbery last night, then, had we?"

Taking a partner with you when filing a complaint with the Law is as bad as taking a child, even if the policeman is extremely good-looking and has a sense of humour. Just don't do it, and especially not in another country, unless you fancy seeing your partner spend the night in a police cell – or possibly yourself.

LOVE AND A TWAT

The only sort of love you'll ever get from a twat will be a large dose of TLC (which is usually used when you are ill or he's done something wrong), jokes made at your own expense, practical help and compliments that are usually far from what you'd like to hear. 'Romance' is just not in his emotional vocabulary.

When I first met my boyfriend, he looked at me and said, "Wow". I understood this to be some sort of dialect from the north and hoped that it meant something positive. This was the occasion that I described earlier in this book (see *Early Days of Twatdom*, Chapter 1), when he presented me with a beautiful book about Cumbria and a kilo of Cumberland sausages, which made me look and feel quite a tit when I walked into the wine bar with them to meet my friends.

Before he moved over here, when I was living alone with the children, I clearly remember one particular evening when we were all sitting in the kitchen having supper and a van drove up outside the house. A man stepped out with a long-stemmed rose, beautifully wrapped, and started approaching the front door. As the children cooed away telling me that I'd been sent a rose, I told them to be quiet – the man must have the wrong house. But as I went to divert the man elsewhere, I realised that the rose was, in fact, addressed to me. My boyfriend had sent me a rose, and considering he's a northerner with absolutely no sense of romance, I was so surprised that I was almost moved to tears.

This did, in fact, happen a second time, at exactly the same time of day and when, once again, I was surrounded by my kids. Timing was never the Twat's strongpoint. The kids certainly didn't make it easy for me. They started making kissing sounds and saying daft things such as, "Mama's in love", which took out just about all of the romance that there was in the gesture. But then, love from afar is never quite the same thing as love when together, where I'm told that I sound like Marge Simpson and am supposed to take it as a compliment.

The Twat's perfect Valentine present for me one year – at least in his mind – was a coil/IUD. Most men buy their loved ones flowers on February 14th, usually, I suspect, as a peace-offering, or simply to make sure that their partner has nothing to moan about for at least a day. I admit that, as a member of the female species, I know that we can be difficult to please at times and it really is best not to try and understand us as we don't want to be understood, just loved and appreciated. But when you're given a coil on Saint Valentine's day, you really have to step back and think twice about what could possibly be going on in your partner's tiny, little mind. Such as:

• He's obviously expecting a shag without the patter of little feet nine months later;

• He definitely doesn't want to hear the patter of little feet at any given time in the near future;

• He's run out of ideas for presents; or

• He recently saw a bumper sticker reading, *Say it with a coil.*

I admit that I gave up trying to work out what made my partner offer me such a gift on Valentine's Day. I simply laughed about it and reckoned that he'd just saved me an awful lot of money. But it's not the most romantic gesture he's made me. He once gave me a tiny bit of some money that he'd inherited so I could buy some new taps for the shower and get it working again. Nice. Oh yes, a twat can surprise you every now and then in the romance stakes, though not necessarily in the manner that you'd like, and of which St Valentine would have approved.

My boyfriend isn't really into 'love', as it were. Maybe it's a northern thing, I don't know, but he's quite happy giving me a slap on the backside and saying, "Awrright, lass?" If your partner is the same and you can live with it, then there's nothing to complain about except at anniversaries. It appears that twats are incapable of giving a decent present and the last birthday present I had from him was €5. I've already spent 98 cents out of that on unpaid postage for a birthday card I was sent that was short of stamps. God knows how far I can stretch the remaining €4.

TWAT HUMOUR

"Knock, knock."

"Cumin... "

My boyfriend has a dual sense of humour. He can come up with the funniest of things, or say something that will leave everybody else looking extremely baffled while he sits there clutching his belly and laughs and laughs and laughs. And he does come out with some of the strangest things. This, for example, is the Twat's method of voting during the Eurovision Song Contest:

Skirt = { (exposed leg length (in inches) – amount (weight in ounces) of material) x transparency of material }

Song = { (number of syllables in lyrics / number of notes) / frequency of chorus }

Awfulness Quotient = { (skirt / song) x number of non-musical gimmicks (acrobats, people in animal costumes etc + number of non-musical people on stage) }

Exposed leg 25
Skirt weight 5
Transparency 5
(That should be pretty skimpy.)

Song syllables 200
Notes 10
Chorus 5
(That should sound pretty awful.)

<u>Extras</u>
non-musical gimmicks 1
non-musical people on stage (dancers, etc) 5
Skirt = { (25 − 5) x 5 } - 100
Song = { (200/10) / 5 } - 5
Awfulness = { (100/5) x (non-musical gimmicks 1 + non musical people 5)
Awfulness = 20 x 5 = 100

I understand very little of what the Twat is trying to say in the above method of voting, as my preferred method of watching the Eurovision Song Contest is to get as plastered as possible. It makes no difference to the actual show as all the songs sound the same anyway, apart from the odd year when some country's performers decide to dress up as a load of zombies.

A lot of the Twat's humour is based around me and it is never terribly complimentary, either. If he cuts himself shaving and somebody remarks on it, he'll shrug it off by saying something along the lines of how hard it is "living with Zoe". This has happened on quite a few occasions over the past few years and I have been the person responsible for having tried to give the man food-poisoning and cause cuts to his hands and face, to name but a few. For some reason, people seem to find these accusations extremely funny and I am often left pondering as to whether or not they actually believe the Twat, as they all walk off laughing at the violence that I have supposedly inflicted upon him.

Then there are those embarrassing moments when I simply wish that I wasn't anywhere near Quarsan. One of these occurred during a visit to the local tip, where the Twat was trying to be as friendly as he could with the man working there.

The Twat carried on, in his friendly way, and the conversation took the following shape.

Man from Tip: "Where are you from?"

Twat: "England, but I'm getting better now. And you?"

Man from Tip: "I'm from Albania – "

" – and I'm Flemish," squeaked the woman who also works at the tip.

Twat: "It's just like Eurovision, ha-ha!"

I stood there, staring at the two people working at the tip who were laughing along with the Twat. Perhaps they were laughing out of courtesy, I considered, as it was quite possible that they didn't even catch on to the Twat's jokes, or even understand them. In order not to make them feel too uncomfortable, I joined in, as is so often the case.

I sometimes worry as to whether or not my sense of humour is getting more like my boyfriend's, but if it makes me and others laugh, then surely it must be good for the soul. Or simply a test as to the virtues of my patience.

Another hobby of my boyfriend's is to change my entire website when I happen to go away for a weekend, or be ill in bed. As he was the one who set up my site, he knows the password and user name to access it, and he takes great delight in changing the pictures and title of the site, as well as posting as much as possible about the subjects that he feels most passionate about, notably: Kylie Minogue, sheds, trebuchets and dubious music. I only have myself to blame, because I know I should change the password every so often, but I always forget. Tweaking my website is something that makes the Twat roll around the floor laughing, as he knows only too well how I will, and always do, react. With frustration and fury.

Here is an example of his handiwork. Earlier this year I spent a weekend with some friends in Holland, which of course gave the Twat an ideal opportunity to play. They happened to look at my website one morning while I was there and discovered that instead of *My Boyfriend Is a Twat*, it was entitled, *My Boyfriend is Lovely*. This title later changed to *Anne Robinson's Evil Twin*, then to *Kleine Belgische* (Little Belgian), and finally to *Michael Owen's Future Wife*. There may have been other title-changes during the day but I was intent on visiting my friends, not spending the entire time in front of their computer reading the strange updates that the Twat kept putting up. This hobby of his keeps him deeply amused and, to be honest, why deprive the man of his sick sense of humour? I even believe that some of my readers found it funny, too, damn them.

My only advice to those of you who end up being made fun of, or teased, is to ask yourself just how much does it bother you? I'm used to it now and being the pretty thick-skinned person that I can be, just grin and bear it. In fact, my boyfriend makes me laugh but if yours doesn't, then it's time to move on. If you don't, you'll only get wrinkles and end up anally retentive.

Only this morning, due to getting a migraine I ended up going back to bed rather than off to work. When I woke up at 1pm, tired, but nevertheless rid of the migraine, I quickly checked my blog and there happened to be a rather nice picture of Kylie up there, under the heading *Madam is Unwell.*

He's *so* predictable.

CLASS TWAT ACTS

I'd like to dedicate this small section to all the things that my boyfriend has either said or done that make me simply roll my eyes and think, "You *twat*!"

Buying presents is something that the Twat is, in general, extremely good at doing. He is incredibly generous towards my children as well as myself, but he has made the odd major blunder. One Christmas, the man decided to buy a new computer monitor to replace mine that had died. He found one on eBay and collected it from the seller who happened to live in Belgium. The monitor was a 22-inch one that had been used by a professional artist who made videos. By the time the monitor was on my small desk, it was almost touching my nose and I had to squint to see anything. It took ages to try and get a clear picture on it and it was quickly evident that my graphics card wasn't up to the job.

Needless to say, I ended up with the Twat's old monitor and he took my 'new' present for himself.

One birthday, the Twat decided to buy me a Zen portable

MP3 player which had so many extra facilities that the only thing that it couldn't do was make me a cup of coffee. I was very impressed, but barely five minutes after having given me the present, he told me, "It will be so useful to us for recording interviews when we go to next year's Al Jazeera conference." I felt very hurt and probably overreacted by giving it back to him. There are some things that are simply better not said.

The evening of the above-mentioned birthday, I was spoilt with the almost traditional birthday meal of steak and chips. We ran out of wine after the meal and so the Twat ventured down to the nearby Night Shop at around 11.15pm. I cleared up and sat back, waiting for his return. At midnight, I turned off all the lights and went to bed. The Twat staggered in four hours later, reeking of beer and smoke as, rather than get a bottle of wine, he had stayed and had several pints in the pub next door.

A clever idea is not always a good one. The Twat and a friend visited Cologne by car, to meet up with some friends there. Not being familiar with the area, or even the country, the Twat decided to take a photograph of the car so that he could remember where it was parked. The trouble was, by the evening he had completely forgotten what area he'd parked the car in, and it was only by sheer luck that one of the German friends was actually a local and recognised the location from the photograph and took them back to the spot.

The Twat is a very careful driver, but I suppose we all have our moments. The first time that he test-drove our friend's car, having never driven on the right-hand side of the road before, was interesting, to say the least. I still say that, as the driver, it was the Twat's fault that we ended up going the wrong way down a one-way street, despite the large sign at the top of the road announcing, in both words and diagram, that it was one-way.

This was closely followed by another incident whereby the following conversation took place.

"Zoe, what is that idiot doing driving straight towards us?"

"Driving, and so are you, *only you're on the wrong side of the road.*"

Seeing through the eyes of the Twat. For some bizarre reason I received an inflatable neck-rest from my bank. The Twat had no idea what it was. They obviously don't exist up north. So I went to great lengths to explain to him exactly what it was for, whereupon he blew it up and here is just one of the things that he used it for...

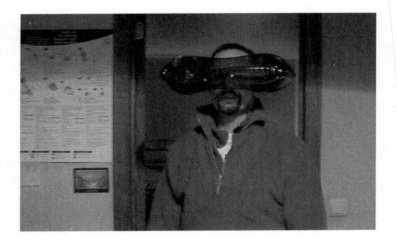

Out of a hat, scarf and sunglasses, not to mention the other uses he suggested, I'll go with the sunglasses.

Communication is not one of the Twat's finest attributes. If he decides to talk to me at all, it is usually in the form of a grunt. He once spent two and a half hours on the phone to his best friend and when he finally came to bed, although dead tired, I asked him how Dan was.

"Owright."

"And Janie?"

"Owright."

"Is that all?"

"Aye."

"That's **all**, after spending that long on the phone?"

"Shurrup an' go to sleep."

There's either a communication break-down here, or "Shurrup an' go to sleep" is the equivalent of "Sweet dreams" up north.

Food obsessions and repetition are two things that the Twat is excellent at, the latter probably occurring in order to make me feel as if he really does talk to me.

During the Twat's first visit to England from here he sent me the following six text messages.

1. *The flapjacks were great.*

2. *Chris has a Rick Astley haircut.*

3. *We're off to have pie and chips now.*

4. *Chris has a Rick Astley haircut.*

5. *We're off to have bangers, mash and peas now.*

6. *Chris has a Rick Astley haircut.*

I find the things that the Twat finds important in his life – apart from food – to be somewhat bizarre. I mean, what's with all the repetition?

When navigating around a city, my boyfriend appears to do so as if standing on top of a mountain. He looks for something on the skyline, then navigates around it as if it were a mountain peak.

The only way that I can get my boyfriend to notice that I have had my hair cut, something which is strangely important to the female species, is to leave my bank card at home. I then call him and ask him if he'd be so kind as to pick me up – and also withdraw some money on the way. It seems to work each time.

Since the Twat took up photography, he spends hours wandering around Brussels, getting extremely lost and yet finding some excellent places/monuments/murals, etc., to photograph. He does tend to get so lost at times that he ends up ringing friends to ask where, exactly, he is.

This applies to children, too, but the Twat will, without fail, put an empty jar back into the fridge. Failing that, he will replace an empty box of sugar, for example, back into the cupboard. He will never buy everything on the shopping list – that is, if he remembers to take it with him – and will always leave the renewal of his asthma prescription up until the very last moment.

TWATTISMS

Twat: *"You have no idea how seriously Zoe is taking her new laptop. She's been lying in bed for the past four days playing on it but what she doesn't realise is that on the top of it it says 'Etch-a-Sketch'."*

"You know, you're a grumpy sod, but I love you."
"And THAT'S meant to make me feel better?"

* * *

"STOP FARTING."
"Think of it as whale-song, darling."

* * *

"You do realise that I make your life as hellish as possible on purpose?"
"Yes, and imagine how bad it would be if I actually listened to you?"

* * *

"Your gaydar is the best since Stevie Wonder's."

* * *

"So how are you feeling, darling?"
"I can't type fast and I feel very confused."
"Ah, well, back to normal then, aren't we?"

"I know, I'm not stupid – I just look it."
"No you don't, you look gorgeous – I've seen your website."

* * *

*"God, if only you had a 'mute' button, my life would
be so much happier."*

* * *

"Please close the window."
"Why?"
"Because I'm cold."
*"Well, try shutting your gob then – you lose 90% of
your body-heat through that."*

* * *

The Twat was just wriggling his mobile phone under
my nose when he asked me:
"Do you know why it's wriggling about?"
"Uh, no."
"Because it's mobile."

"Oh Christ, I need a boob-lift."
"Why don't you just get the rest of your body lowered?"

* * *

Talking about my website: *"But you can hardly see the
eggs in the photo."*
"Your screen must be lighter than mine."
"People will have to squint to see them."
**"That way you know that people are reading your
blog closely."**

* * *

*"You know, it's a good job that I don't 'go for looks' –
you're ugly as pigshit, but your personality is what I love."*
**"Well, it's a good job that that's the same way that I
feel about you – there's only one woman in this
household that I think is gorgeous."**
"Who is that?"
"Kylie, on her DVD."

"But the bread's stale and you don't want to get some more.
Never mind, I'll starve to death."
"Well, that will take a long time."

* * *

"Stop squeezing my bum."
"Why?"
"Because I said so."
"I'm not squeezing your bum – where is it?"
"Behind me."
"How far back should I look?"

* * *

My son: *"Mama, if I had my stick –"*
Me: *"You don't use sticks in aikido."*
Twat: **"Jake, the only stick you need right now is your tooth-brush. Stick it in your mouth and wriggle it around a bit."**

* * *

"Oh shit, I think I've put my bra on back-to-front."
"That's alright, hon, just turn your tits around."

"I bought Zoe this book on 'How to do Just About Everything'. It's only got one page which says, 'Zoe, just sit there and get everyone else to do everything for you.'"

* * *

Friend: *"I was holding her breast."*
Twat: *"I thought you were pulling up her socks."*

* * *

"Did you know that your shirt's on inside-out?"
"I know, it's the new way of wearing it – for the second week."

* * *

"Listen, why can't you just say 'no' instead of grunting all the time?"
"I can say it, but it's just getting you to listen."

"You have no idea what it's like being me, dear."
"Oh thank God for that, at least I've been spared that one."

* * *

**"I'm so glad that you recognise your children, darling.
Perhaps they can take their name badges off now."**

* * *

"Hon, why do you look like a hamster chewing a wasp?"

* * *

"It feels like my wisdom tooth has popped up."
"Well, it might 'uv done."
"Yes, but wouldn't that hurt? And I can't shut my jaw properly."
"When did you last try?"

* * *

"No – you can't wear those pants, you wore them yesterday."
"Yes, but it was a good day, so I'll wear them again today."

"Did you know that you've gone through more mobile phones during the two and a half years that you've been here than I ever have."
"Oh, that's due to all the hot and steamy SMS's that I send."
"True. You do send a lot…"
"Not to you I don't."

* * *

"Oh bugger, I almost fell up the stairs."
"Well now, there's a change in direction."

* * *

"Quarsan, you're not wearing those again today."
"Why not?"
"Because you love me, don't you?"
"Yes, but not enough to change my pants."

* * *

"Do you mind if I slide down the stairs?"
"Darling, I'm more used to you pouring yourself down the stairs."

"I bought a book all about feng shui yesterday."
"Oh really?"
"I brought it home but I didn't know where to put it."

* * *

"You know, darling, I'm not sure about going to Paris on
my own."
"Why not? You could take Sue to the Musée d'Orsay."
"Hell no – you know what I'm like – I'd get lost."
"Zoe, you never get lost. I've been asking you to for the
past three years."

* * *

"Ooh, darling, you've been here for almost two and a half
years now. I obviously have this magnetic attraction."
"You certainly do, darling. Shame none of it is positive."

* * *

"Q, I think you've lost your sense of humour."
"Yes, I'm turning into a feminist."

"Jake pulled out your bottle of vodka and asked if it was water. Luckily I still have enough decent moral standards to say 'no'."

* * *

"I met someone from my Belgian class just now."
"Oh right, who was that?"
"Well, I didn't really recognise her at first because she was wearing these huge dark glasses. But I told her I was looking for my girlfriend."
"Eh?"
"She's Italian, you see."
"Oh. Italian. Dark glasses – how was she dressed?"
"Well, I dunno. Clothes."

* * *

As I snuggled up in bed last night I noticed, not for the first time, the strong smell of nicotine coming from the Twat's direction.
"Christ, it's like going to bed with a fag."
"Why? I'm totally straight."

"*I was just thinking…*"
"Oh Christ, don't you remember what happened the last time?"

* * *

"*When did I call Dan?*"
"Last night when I was learning how to speak Belgian."
"*Oh Christ. No.*"
"You did, he called me to say so."
"*What did you tell him?*"
"Zoe + alcohol + PMS = chaos."

* * *

"*For goodness' sake, sweetie, it'll be alright. I'm your mother.*"
"Well, that's not a very nice thing to tell your daughter."

* * *

"*Coffee? That dehydrates you.*"
"If that's the case, then I should be a cream cracker by now."

"Tell me, how does it feel when a bloke has an orgasm?"
"I dunno. I'll let you know when I have one."

* * *

"Damn it. You never think of me, do you?"
"Yes, but as little as possible."

* * *

"Don't you think you have a big problem?"
"Yes, but there's not a lot I can do about you, hon."

* * *

"Why do you keep looking at my arse?"
"Because I'm sick of looking at your face."

* * *

The Twat was replying to an email from a female friend who said, *'If logic would have it, men would ride sidesaddle'*. I thought that was a very valid point until I saw the Twat's reply, which said, *'**And women wouldn't sit on washing machines.**'*

"Why is my son dressed up in cowboy trousers and an Indian top?"
"Because he's playing cowboys and Indians."
*"But he's dressed up in cowboy trousers **AND** an Indian top. It doesn't make sense."*
"Yes it does. Maybe he's bi-western."

* * *

"I only feel like groping you because of society's pressure to conform to outmoded gender rules and expectations."

* * *

"I never have that problem, love, because I believe in letting out good, long farts."
(Don't I know it.)
"These farts are excellent for muscular movement around my stomach and bowels, so I've never suffered in that area. Farting like I do stretches my abdomen and is excellent in that I don't ever suffer from stomach ailments."

"How can you miss your mouth? It's the biggest thing on you."

* * *

"If you could find an example of you showing your love for me, that would be nice."
"I've got a Kylie DVD."

* * *

As I looked out of the window with the Twat at two (I think) of my kids making a snowman, I asked him why the hell they had one large head for the snowman and one tiny one. The Twat looked at me, worryingly, then said:
"That's the football, darling."

* * *

"Quarsan, I'm the one who wears the trousers in this household."
"And I'm the one who wears the tracksuit bottoms."
"What I mean is, I'm the one who gives the orders."
"And I'm the one who ignores them."

With regard to those huge satellite dishes that I hate so much:
"Size matters – but it depends on the reception you get."

* * *

"I was thinking."
"Oh, that's what it is. I thought you were in real pain."

* * *

We were once sitting in our local restaurant and, after having read our coffee dregs, I noticed the beautiful baby that someone had brought in. Most babies are ghastly, but this one had huge, bright blue eyes, smiled at the few stragglers left in the restaurant and was very quiet. I told the Twat that our baby would look just like that, to which he replied: *"No it wouldn't, it would have a goatee and run around saying 'wow' a lot."*
A bit later: *"My baby would look just like that."*
"Mine wouldn't. He'd be waving his legs around, giggling at his own farts and saying 'Eh up, Mama'."

"Will you stop leaning against me – what is it with you all, you lean against me. It's like living with a load of dogs."
"You know why? Because you're barking." And then the Twat clutched his belly and laughed and laughed
– and laughed.

* * *

As I was speaking to a friend over Skype, even the Twat could hear the poor girl coughing and so shouted into my headphones: **"Get it out lass, better out than in! Think of it as your throat farting."**

* * *

I was talking to a friend over Skype and I didn't quite catch what she said – and then the Twat joined in...
Me: *"Tim Buck?"*
TT: **"He's a twin, you know."**
Me: *"Eh? How do you know?"*
TT: **"Ever heard of 'Tim Buck Two'?"**

"I want the Twat to have a look at it because if I look at it one more time I'll go loopy."
"Well, we'll put that down as one of the world's longest journeys..."

* * *

"Oooo, yes, I must look out for a Dangermouse DVD on Ebay."
"No, Quarsan, you can't. It's stupid."
"What's stupid about it? He's the greatest, he's fantastic, wherever there is danger, he'll be there."
"It's still stupid – what's so great about a cartoon mouse dressed in spandex?"
"It's not stupid – he even does a little dance before he goes off."
"A 'little dance' ? A spandex-clad mouse dancing and then saving the world? Rubbish."
"Well, it was the '80s, and besides, haven't you ever heard of Spandex Ballet?"

"I was born on Wednesday which means I'm full of grace."
"Well, I was born on a Monday meaning that I'm fair of face."
"So what day were people born 'wide of arse' then?"

* * *

"Quarsan, I DO care."
"Don't worry darling, I won't tell anyone."

* * *

I was pissed off when, just because my son had missed two
swimming lessons in a row at school, I got a message from
his teacher saying, *'Your son would need a medical
certificate'*. WTF? The little tyke isn't even earning and he
needs a medical certificate? The Twat came up with the
solution. *"Just tell his teacher that he's soluble."*

* * *

"And I've got a lovely bottle of wine for you, Zoe."
"Oh great – you'd better let it breathe for ages."
"Yes – that's the big difference between wine and children."

Twats —
The Last Word

FREQUENTLY ASKED QUESTIONS

I am often asked questions about the Twat and so one day I decided to put up a post on my website encouraging readers to ask questions to which my dear Partner would reply. Then I started getting worried as I already knew the answers and knew that I wouldn't be spared any compassion. We decided to tape the Q&A session. I asked the questions, he answered. As it took almost an hour to do the entire lot, you can hear me getting more and more inebriated as I struggled to pronounce words and stay on the sofa.

What did people ask? What were the answers? Just read on...

Q: How are the newts?
A: The newts are *just* fine.

Q: How do you cope with Zoe?
A: Mmmm, how do I cope with Zoe? It's a combination of ignoring her as much as possible and, really, repeating the phrase that pays: "Yes, dear."

Q: When you first met her kids, did you ever say to yourself, "What the hell am I getting myself into?" (Literally.)
A: I did say that, but in reference to Zoe and not the kids. I first met the kids when I first moved over here and I remember that they seemed very polite and that they were really easy. The easiest aspect of moving over here and in with Zoe was the kids, right from day one. They were great.

Q: What attracted you to Zoe the most?
A: She's just gorgeous. Zoe is very funny and just ... amiably nuts.

Q: Does Zoe calling you the Twat make you smile?
A: Not really, I get used to it. I get called it 50 to 60 times a day, so, you know...

Q: If you had to change anything about Zoe what would it be? (Careful.)
A: The volume.

Q: Why do you live with me? (Yes, I asked that.)
A: There's a theory that I'm paying for a sin in a past life, but you know, we get on – it's cool. Life's fine – I'm mad about Zoe and Zoe's mad.

Q: Why are you living with my horrible mum? She's crazy. (Jake asked this one.)
A: Jake, I'm doing this for two reasons. One, to protect you, and secondly, as I always say, I suffer so that other men may live free.

Q: If you had to be on 'Twats in Their Eyes', who would you be and what would you sing?
A: I'd probably sing *Peace in the Valley* by the Alabama 3.

Q: Do you wear armour and play loud music in your earphones when Zoe talks to you?
A: No. I just kind of filter it out, it's a bit like static, background radiation.

Q: Do you answer back or do you fear retaliation? (Holiday in the dog house.)
A: As I said before, I use the phrase that pays a lot.

Q: Why do you have a house in Tanzania but live in Belgium? And don't just blame it on Zoe...
A: It's not Zoe's fault. I have this house in a village on loan from the village government, which is very kind of them, and

why not have a house in Tanzania? One day, *Inshallah*, we'll go and live there.

Q: Do you still have the poncy poofy tracky trainers? Are you allowed to wear them in public?
A: I have and I do.

Q: Maybe Zoe should put them on eBay...
A: If they'd make any money, I could then go ahead and buy some more from Ron Hill. Online.

Q: What is the answer to life, the universe and everything?
A: The answer to that is quite simple, it's 42. Everyone knows that.

Q: And where did I leave my bloody coat?
A: I think you'll find that it's probably behind the sofa. (It was, we later learned.)

Q: Is little Quickos still alive?
A: Little Quickos still lives with us and will get back to blogging one day. He's happy and alive and still loves everyone. (*www.quarsan.net/quickos*)

Q: Do you mind her calling you a twat? What do you call her?

A: I don't mind at all. I think the thing is that, with all appearances to the contrary, we're very comfortable and settled with each other and I don't take any offence about that. What do I call Zoe? I call her gorgeous.

Q: What happened to Jake's blog?

A: Jake deleted it to annoy his mum. I don't know quite how that worked, but that's how that happened.

Q: Are we ever going to see a YouTube video of you (Quarsan) busting some funky moves?

A: I think you'll find that I'm already there, somewhere, but I'm not going to say where. But I have plenty of funky moves and can bust like a bastard.

Q: If a dog and a monkey got in a fight, which one would win?

A: It entirely depends on what sort of dog and what sort of monkey. Now, you can put a poodle against a chimp and the chimp will always win, but if you got something like a Great Dane, that would probably see off a chimp, and if you're looking for something more like an orang-utan, that could see off most things, actually. In general, dogs have speed and monkeys have strength. It also depends on the fact that they all fight in different ways: monkeys reach out and hit with their arms, whereas dogs use their mouths and try to rip throats out, so it really does depend. You're going to have to be a bit more precise.

Q: Is Zoe's blog ever going back to its original attractive shade of orange?
A: It probably isn't, and pink suits her well.

Q: What is the correct footwear to go with the poncy poofy tracky trainers?
A: Well, you see, I'm a great fan of New Balance, a good Cumbrian design. I've spent many happy years wandering over the fells in their fell runner trainers, so I'd go for anything that are trainers. I'm not one for sandals, or anything like that, but you know, that sort of thing. I wouldn't go for anything too branded, either.

Q: Imagine you could be any anthropod for a day. What would it be and why?

A: Well, first I'd have to figure out what the hell an anthropod is, but I'd like to be a marmoset for a day, that'd be great. I'd be a good meerkat, too. You can picture it, I'd be great.

Q: *Why do aliens only abduct drunken rednecks?*
A: Because they're easy to catch.

Q: *Why do bad things happen to good people?*
A: Bad things happen to all people, good or bad or indifferent.

Q: *Why do birds suddenly appear?*
A: Possibly because you're taking some sort of hallucinogenic.

Q: *Why can't I seem to spell any more?*
A: Because you've been using Spell-checker for so long that you've forgotten your grasp of basic English.

Q: *How is the shed coming along?*
A: Let's just say that it's an ongoing project: one day my shed will come.

Q: *What colour are you going to paint the satellite dishes?*
A: Plum, like the supposed colour of Zoe's site.

Q: Did you find the toenail clippings in your dinner last night, or couldn't you tell?
A: There weren't any toenail clippings in it because, as always, I cooked it. There may have been some in Zoe's, but I couldn't possibly comment.

Q: Is your belly button and innie or an outie?
A: It's an 'innie'.

Q: Will you go see Spandau Ballet if they reform?
A: No, I won't. In fact, I actually remember seeing them in Edinburgh, many, many years ago, just before they got started and signed up. They were tipped as the next coming thing and were doing some secret, prestigious gigs. I went to see them and I thought they were flouncing around in big girls' blouses and was not impressed. So I saw them before they even got a contract. It's not really my thing – I'm not a New Romantic – can you imagine me with Big Hair?

Q: Why on Earth do you have a thing for Kylie Minogue? You have Zoe, or at least I assume you do, what more could you want?
A: All I can say to that is because She's There. She's Kylie.

She's Great. She's Magnificent. If you don't understand, then I'm sorry. You either get it or you don't.

Q: Did you really introduce yourself to people at the meeting last week or whenever, saying: "Hello. I'm the Twat"?
A: Yes I did, and there's a really weird sort of cachet about this. I was at an Al Jazeera conference in Doha, just over a year ago, and I was speaking with a man called Ethan Zucherman who founded Global Voices. He was one of the people who set up Tripod – if you've been on the internet long enough, you'll know who they are – and he's a lovely, lovely man and we were chatting about blogging and all sorts of stuff like that. Then I mentioned Zoe's blog and said that it was about me. He told me he knew about her blog, then said that he had to leave for a minute. He got up from the table and rushed out of the room and came across my best friend, Dan, reached up to him, grabbed him by both shoulders and yelled, "I've met the Twat!" I mentioned this to a lovely former *Guardian* journalist called Julia, who told me she could believe it because she goes around at parties and says, "I've met the Twat." So yeah, I did that. What the hell.

Q: Quarsan, is it at all possible for you to wander around the city

in which you have lived for several years without phoning me up because you're lost? (This came from another Belgian Blogger.)
A: Actually, I didn't phone you up because I was lost, I phoned you up because I was beginning to think I knew where I was, and where I thought I was seemed to be near to where you live. So I mentioned the church round the corner from your place and frankly, you didn't even recognise the name of the church, which is a big one and a well-known one. I have another weblog called Mannekin Pics (*http://www.mannekinpics.blogspot.com*) where I post a different photo of Brussels every day. So I buy a day-pass which allows me to use all the trams, buses and metros for a day and get off at random stops and just wander around taking pictures and I do tend to end up thoroughly lost.

Q: Prior to my next birthday party, will you please remind me to buy a loaf of bread and some bacon in advance so you don't have to pop out and get some the morning after?
A: One thing that I have always known is the importance of bacon. Bacon has got me through so many difficult times in life, in particular the morning after there has been some alcohol consumed. And the morning after Tippler's birthday party, I woke up before any of the others (NOT TRUE!) and

saw several people in dire need of bacon, so I went out to buy some and made some bacon sandwiches. Dan's major claim to fame is that no matter how hungover he is in the morning, he can do a full cooked breakfast for up to 20 people, even when he is so hungover he literally can't speak. I've always taken the Hunter S. Thompson view that if you get your breakfast right, then the rest of your day falls into place. So breakfast, especially bacon, is so important to me.

Q: Where have you hidden Zoe's cleavage?
A: It's right here.

Q: Would you rather live where you are, or in the too-beautiful-for-words Lake District from whence you hail?
A: There are times when I find Belgium really difficult to live in because, well, it's a lovely place and it has a *beautiful* capital city, but administratively, it's a complete mess. I lived for many years in Ambleside in the Lake District, and I just loved it there. I knew everyone in the village, we'd always leave our doors open, the post office or the newsagents was 50 yards away but it could take me two hours to buy a newspaper because I'd always be bumping into so many people and having a chat, and I really, really miss that. I mean, we

live in a road with eight houses and I've only been invited into one person's house. People say that the English are very cold and all that, but my God, the Belgians... I think the Lake District is the most beautiful place in the world. I've travelled widely, but nothing makes my heart sing like the fells and the Lake District.

Q: Would you ever move back to the UK? And if you would, could you convince Zoe to come with you 'cos it's all about her, right?

A: I would love to go back to the Lake District – to me, it's the only habitable place in the United Kingdom, I just feel so comfortable there. Although it's by no means perfect. I've always said that if you live in the Lake District you've got to get out, and often, and that's one of the reasons that I've done so much travelling, and also, it's *incredibly* wet. I used to work on the fells and the mountains and it used to rain all the bloody time and it just makes you so *miserable*, but when you've got a half-decent or a nice day in the Lake District and you happen to be on one of the Lakeland fells, it is one of the most beautiful and perfect places to be. You just feel honoured and privileged to be there. I have so many memories of my days walking and climbing on the Lake District that are just so precious to me. But Zoe can't go back, so we'll be staying here. On the other hand, a bit of peace and quiet is quite tempting...

Q: *What is the meaning of the universe?*
A: There is no meaning to the universe, there is no meaning at all. It's just there, where everyone is.

Q: *What do you think of Americans, really? The ones in the US, if you want to get politically correct.*
A: I've always been a long-time critic of American foreign policy. I've always been very dismissive of American politicians and presidents, but most of the Americans I have met have been very open people, very friendly people, in some ways almost naïve and innocent. The idea of the loudmouth – you know, the stereotype – really doesn't exist. It may exist in America, but I've never been there. I've only met Americans who have travelled, or whatever, and I've found a lot of them to be, in general, just really cool people. Many of the Americans I know are very concerned about the state of America. They're worried that America is becoming intolerant, that it's becoming something un-American, rather than small-time, welcoming, friendly, helpful, live and let live – that it's

becoming something very different. I also met a lot of Americans in Tanzania when the Peace Corps came in and I thought they were very nice people. To be blunt, they appeared rather clueless about the outside world and were suffering from culture shock. But some of them have definitely been some of the most fantastic people I have ever met.

Q: What's the strangest food you've ever tried?
A: I've had a rat-burger in Scotland and I've eaten loads of strange stuff in Africa. When you're invited in to eat by an African, you just can't refuse. Probably the single strangest item that I have ever eaten, and God knows how I recognised it, but I did, was at the wedding of a very good friend of mine in Africa. I was sat at the top table next to my friend and his wife. The funny thing about Tanzania is that you've got to be serious at your wedding to show that you are taking it seriously. You mustn't smile or laugh or anything, you've got to be absolutely deadpan. My friend just couldn't stop smiling. He was so happy that he was finally marrying this girl that he was smiling all the time, you know, and then the food came out and it was this big stew. I put my spoon into it and pulled it out and recognised what it was. I had to eat it because everyone was watching me. I ate a goat's arsehole.

The second incident involving strange food occasion happened in Preston. There was a huge fair called 'The Countryside Comes to Town', with loads of stalls and obviously the National Trust had one, too, showing off the rural walls and paths that people like me help maintain. Whilst sitting at the stall, I got talking to someone who lived in the next valley to me. He was one of the few people who had to be disciplined for having taken a rifle into work because whenever he was out dry-stone walling and saw something that moved, he'd shoot it, take it home and cook it. We got onto the subject of the animals that we'd eaten, as he used to go to Tanzania and stay with a Masaai camp for a couple of weeks. So there we were, listing all the unusual creatures we'd eaten such as zebra, giraffe, elephant, gazelle, and how the dishes had been prepared, when the Head Warden suddenly came rushing over and said, "Would you two fuckin' shurrup, we're the National Trust and meant to be conservationists and you two buggers have eaten every single endangered species on the planet!"

Q: What's the cutest thing you've ever seen?
A: It's that picture of that llama that has been entirely shaved apart from its head.

Q: What makes you proud?
A: Zoe, her blog, the acclaim that she has rightly received, the fact that she has got a book deal – Zoe's written this book and it's fucking *brilliant*. Er... what else? Standing on top of a mountain in the Lake District. It makes me proud to be in a world that has such things.

Q: Should Bossy repaint her shutters or go with the terracotta?
A: Repaint yer shutters.

Q: If Chuck Norris and I [Jack Bauer] got into a brawl, who would win?
A: Personally, I think Jack would win because, quite frankly, Jack is a dirtier fighter than Chuck is, and let's face it, there's something very stiff and wooden about Chuck. I think Jack Bauer would take the fucker down.

Q: What makes you tick, and what are your ambitions in life?
A: My ambition in life is to survive. What makes me tick? I have absolutely no idea, I just, you know... I just get through the day, then another one happens, that's it. Don't look for anything particularly deep in me, arright, lass?

Q: Belgium is flat. Do you hope to climb any mountains?
A: I did do a bit of climbing but the problem is that it's all limestone here, and I don't like limestone – it just doesn't have the character and atmosphere that granite has.

Q: Did you leave the last blogmeet offended, or had you really had a tough day?
A: No, not at all, I was rather inebriated and I have this wonderful survival mechanism that at some point my primal mind kicks in and says, "You are completely pissed, go home NOW." And that's what I do.

Q: Was it love at first sight?
A: That's an interesting question. I was absolutely struck by meeting Zoe and seeing her for the first time. It was as if I was hit by a thunderbolt. So, probably, the answer is – 'yes'.

Q: Do you share Zoe's love of red wine and who out the two of you has the greater capacity for it?
A: I do enjoy a nice glass of red wine, and as for the capacity, let's just say that while recording all this Zoe has already drunk a bottle and half of wine – and I'm just halfway through my second glass.

Q: Did you ever dig out the dinosaur that I sent you?
A: Oh absolutely. You sent me this lovable, lovely little block of – I don't know, something or other, and you had to chip away at it and excavate your own dinosaur, and Quickos and I spent a couple of happy hours digging it out. So yes, we did.

Q: When Zoe isn't around, do you sometimes, secretly, you know, just for the fun and the thrill of it, try on the tiara?
A: No. When Zoe's not around I tend to make the most of my time just chilling out, relaxing and not being stressed.

Q: What music makes the hairs at the back of your neck stand on end?
A: There are some things that do that and one of them is Pretty Vacant, by the Sex Pistols. It just brings a lot of my youth back and it's a stunning, stunning track.

Q: I'd love to know more about your Northern background and any climbing you've done and stuff like that. Go on – spill the beans! My grandad came from Cleator Moor.
A: That is in Yorkshire, which is an inferior county (!) to Lancashire and Cumbria. Most of my climbs have been on the fells of the Lake District. I'm not a particularly 'hard

climber' or anything like that, I've done a lot of the traditional routes in the Lake District, and I just love it. I love the different perspective you get, the different view you get, the idea that you look upon a crag as a puzzle where you're using your hands, your brain, your strength, your intelligence to really gerrup and get there and be a part of the mountain environment. You are so much more engaged with the mountain environment if you're climbing than if you're just walking on the fells.

Apart from that, I've done a lot of winter ice-climbing in Scotland. I love Ben Nevis and had a great time climbing Zero Gulley and Tollow Ridge and various others. The best single day out that I have ever had on a mountain was with a friend of mine on the Isle of Skye, climbing the Cuillin Ridge. It was a beautiful summer's day and we just wore shorts and had very little equipment and we went along there as fast as we could and it was just fantastic. I've done a little bit of climbing in Africa and other places, and a little bit in the Alps which I found a bit too commercial. I'd rather have the Cumbrian attitude towards mountaineering where you don't use bolts, you don't use anything artificial, it's all about being a part of the environment.

Q: Are you a high maintenance twat? What does Zoe do for you that's extra special?

A: I'm zero-maintenance, really. I require no maintenance whatsoever.

(He wasn't allowed to answer the next part of the question.)

Q: Why are you THE Twat, not just any twat but the Twat? And when was the first time Zoe called you so?

A: I am THE Twat. All the others are inferior and are, quite frankly, carbon copies. I think that the first time that Zoe called me a twat was probably within two seconds of us meeting.

Q: Quarsan, are you good at telling porkies?

A: I am absolutely FANTASTIC.

Q: If you are doing a podcast, will you be signing off with a big 'tooodle-pip'?

A: I have no idea how to toodle-pip. Perhaps someone can give me instructions as to how to toodle-pip?

WHAT ARE MEN LIKE?

I have a good friend to thank for sending me this list of male characteristics, most of which fit the Twat to a T.

Men are like... Laxatives.
They irritate the crap out of you.

Men are like... Bananas.
The older they get, the less firm they are.

Men are like... Weather.
Nothing can be done to change them.

Men are like... Blenders.
You need one, but you're not quite sure why.

Men are like... Chocolate Bars.
Sweet, smooth, and they usually head straight for your hips.

Men are like... Commercials.
You can't believe a word they say.

Men are like... Department Stores.
Their clothes are always half off!

Men are like... Government Bonds.
They take *soooooooo* long to mature.

Men are like... Mascara.
They usually run at the first sign of emotion.

Men are like... Popcorn.
They satisfy you, but only for a little while.

Men are like... Snowstorms.
You never know when they're coming, how many inches you'll get, or how long it will last.

Men are like... Lava Lamps.
Fun to look at, but not very bright.

Men are like... Parking Spots.
All the good ones are taken, the rest are disabled.

QUIZ

IS YOUR BOYFRIEND A TWAT?

Tick each of the following statements that applies to your man. Add them up at the end and find out if your boyfriend is a true twat, or just displaying the early symptoms.

1. He cringes when you acquire the complete series of *Desperate Housewives* and says, "Well, that's one thing you won't catch me watching." Two days later you find him glued to the telly, completely addicted to the series.

2. You ask your boyfriend to design your website and find that he takes it over as soon as you leave the house by transforming it into his own 'Kylie Fan Club' and a place to discuss all his favourite interests.

3. When you ask him to do something, you find that it never gets done, despite the Post-it notes left all around the house as a reminder.

4. When your boyfriend decides to buy something for himself, he goes to any lengths to get it, even if it means leaving the country.

5. Whenever he comes to bed after you, he slams the bedroom door, turns on the light and makes as much noise as possible.

6. If he comes home drunk, you know you're better off sleeping in another bedroom – or even another house.

7. He leaves empty plates of food, coffee mugs and glasses all over the house and never clears them away.

8. He eats everything in the fridge and replaces the empty pots and wrappers in the false belief that you'll think the food is still there.

9. He complains that the house looks untidy, but won't admit that the mess is his, and certainly won't clear up.

10. His best friend is his computer.

11. His favourite bed companion is a soft toy, or even the dog, rather than you.

12. Whenever you lose your temper, your boyfriend always blames it on PMS.

13. He tells you how wonderful he is and lists his great qualities, none of which you've ever spotted in him.

14. He gets on with anybody and everybody, even the most unlikely of people, such as tramps and people who haunt garbage tips.

15. He leaves everything turned on – the lights, the TV, the radio – and frequently leaves the freezer, fridge or front door open.

16. When drunk, your boyfriend will find himself a comfy bed, leaving you stranded wherever you may be, even if that means comatose on the living room rug.

17. He uses the shed for anything other than its proper purpose. As a bar, a TV room, an internet café, even a bedroom.

18. The only pairs of trousers he owns are tracksuit bottoms.

19. He is incapable of any form of DIY more complex than banging a nail into the wall.

20. His idea of a romantic gesture is a slap on your backside.

Score:

0 – 5: Your boyfriend may express twat tendencies from time to time but, actually, he's rather dull.

6 – 10: Your boyfriend is on the road to twatdom, resorting to twattish behaviour under pressure.

11 – 15: I would start getting worried.

16 and over: Congratulations. Your boyfriend is a twat.

Index

Note: page numbers in **bold** refer to photographs.

Index

Index